THE ORVIS
GUIDE TO
Upland Hunting

THE ORVIS
GUIDE TO
Upland Hunting

REID BRYANT

Photography by Brian Grossenbacher
Foreword by Simon Perkins

Essex, Connecticut

An imprint of Globe Pequot, the trade division of
The Rowman & Littlefield Publishing Group, Inc.
4501 Forbes Blvd., Ste. 200
Lanham, MD 20706
www.rowman.com

Distributed by NATIONAL BOOK NETWORK

First Lyons Press paperback edition 2024
Text copyright © 2017 Reid Bryant
Foreword copyright © 2017 Simon Perkins

All photographs copyright © 2017 Brian Grossenbacher, except pages 66 and 71, which are copyright © John Skinner.

All rights reserved. No part of this book may be reproduced in any form or by any electronic or mechanical means, including information storage and retrieval systems, without written permission from the publisher, except by a reviewer who may quote passages in a review.

British Library Cataloguing in Publication Information available

Library of Congress Cataloging-in-Publication Data

Library of Congress Catalog Control Number: 2017937195

ISBN: 9781493084036 (paperback)
ISBN: 9781493084043 (electronic)
ISBN: 9780789327741 (cloth)

Printed in India

I dedicate this book to Dave Brown
and Dave Linck of Craftsbury, Vermont. They taught me
about grouse and woodcock, hardwood smoke and chewing tobacco,
and how nothing is so lovely as a Vermont October, when the
apple crop is good and the popples on Ketchum Hill have gone to gold.

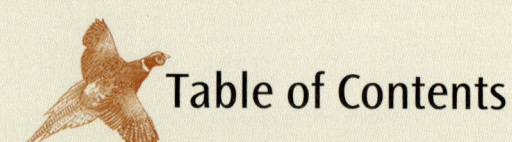

Table of Contents

Foreword
by Simon Perkins 10

Introduction
by Reid Bryant 15

Chapter 1 24
THE WHAT AND THE WHY

Chapter 2 32
A BRIEF HISTORY

Chapter 3 40
WHAT WE ARE AFTER
- 44 ■ Grouse
- 45 ■ Pheasant
- 46 ■ Partridge
- 49 ■ Quail
- 49 ■ Woodcock
- 51 ■ Doves
- 52 ■ In Summary

Chapter 4 54
GUNS AND SHOOTING
- 58 ■ Ammunition
  - ■ Gauge
  - ■ Length
  - ■ Shot Size
  - ■ Powder Charge
  - ■ Other Terms
- 63 ■ Anatomy of a Shotgun
  - ■ Barrels
  - ■ Action
  - ■ Stock
- 79 ■ Decisions, Decisions
- 82 ■ Practicality and Necessity:
  The Legal Aspects
  - ■ Gun Laws
  - ■ Game and Hunting Laws
  - ■ The Preserve Option

Chapter 5 86
DRESSING THE PART
- 90 ■ Boots
- 93 ■ Pants
- 95 ■ Chaps
- 97 ■ Shirts
- 99 ■ Vests
- 102 ■ Jackets
- 103 ■ Accessories
  - ■ Hats
  - ■ Glasses
  - ■ Hearing Protection
  - ■ Gloves
  - ■ Other Accessories

Chapter 6 108
WHERE TO HUNT
- **113** ■ The Preserve Option
- **116** ■ Public vs. Private Land
  - Private Land Access
  - Public Land Access
- **122** ■ Where Might I Find the Birds?
  - The Humanistic Approach
  - The Academic Approach

Chapter 7 130
DOGS
- **137** ■ Pointing Breeds
  - English Pointer
  - English Setter
  - Gordon Setter
  - Irish, Red, or Red-and-White Setter
  - German Shorthaired Pointer
  - German Wirehaired Pointer, Wirehaired Pointing Griffon, and Deutsch Drahthaar
  - American and French Brittany
  - Vizsla
  - Weimeraner
  - Less-Common Breeds
- **154** ■ Flushing Breeds
  - English Springer Spaniel
  - English Cocker Spaniel
  - Boykin Spaniel
  - Labrador Retriever
  - Other Breeds
- **163** ■ A Few More Thoughts on Dogs

Chapter 8 164
INTO THE FIELD
- **168** ■ Prior Planning
- **173** ■ The Meet-Up
- **178** ■ Let 'Em See You Shoot
- **179** ■ Load Up and Go
- **183** ■ Bird Up, Bird Down
- **187** ■ The Wrap-Up
- **188** ■ Birds Down
  - Use Enough Gun
  - Shoot within Your Limits
  - Cripples

Chapter 9 196
PREPPING GAME BIRDS FOR THE TABLE
- **201** ■ Field Dressing
- **203** ■ Plucking, Skinning, and Breasting
- **207** ■ Hanging and Aging
- **209** ■ Incidentals
- **209** ■ Taxidermy
- **216** ■ A Conservation Conversation

Chapter 10 222
SUNDRIES
- **225** ■ Doves
- **227** ■ Driven Bird Shooting
- **232** ■ Sporting Clays

Afterword 238
Glossary 244
Acknowledgments 256

Foreword

I am not the right person to be writing this foreword.

I like to think of myself as someone who strives to appreciate all experiences in life, even the familiar and ordinary. I was raised by a family that kept bird dogs in the house, ate grouse and quail for dinner, and handed down double shotguns from great-grandmother to grandfather to father to son. I like to believe that from the beginning I saw my life in upland hunting as unique and desirable, and consciously celebrated it despite its steady and significant presence. But to be honest, I took my "upland upbringing" for granted.

Upland hunting surrounded me as a kid. On October weekends, as my brother and I cleared our breakfast dishes from the table, I would sneak odds and ends to our black Lab Alis and our English pointer Glider before the dogs would rush outside to prance around the cars in the driveway. Before long, my dad would come out of the house with his shotgun, hunting vest, and faded orange hat. Being too young to join them, I would watch my dad load Alis and Glider into the back of his red jeep and then wave as he drove down the driveway to explore his favorite southern Vermont grouse woods. When the three of them returned, if my dad had been successful, I would run around the yard hiding his grouse in different piles of leaves so I could "work the dogs." I now fully appreciate the patience with which Alis would indulge my dog trainer impersonations. I would repeatedly mimic my dad's hand signals as I told her to *sit* and *stay*, then run off to stash the bird in a challenging spot before telling her to *go fetch*! Her enthusiasm for this game never waned, as she repeatedly worked her nose through clumps of dry leaves, bringing the bird back to me again and again until I got bored, distracted, or called inside for dinner.

These childhood rituals were constant. Throughout the autumn, in between soccer games and playtime with friends, my dad and uncle would make time to throw clay targets for me and my brother in the meadow across the river, helping us meticulously practice safe and effective gun handling in the field. Each Thanksgiving or New Year's we visited my grandfather's house in the longleaf pine woods of North Florida, where we hunted bobwhite quail every morning and afternoon and

by SIMON PERKINS

ended the days with post-dinner naps on the floor next to bird dogs. And at each Christmas, the most meaningful presents under the tree were always identified by a card with a grouse feather affixed with melted candle wax.

I guess my immersion in upland hunting might best compare to the experience of a child learning a second language from bilingual parents. The dialect is always around them, humming either in the forefront or background, and it is absorbed at an early enough age that they never fully appreciate the efforts, struggles, and defining moments of the indoctrination. This book's foreword should have been written by someone who could artfully document the intricate journey of "discovering" upland hunting. For better or for worse, that's not me.

But my perspective on upland hunting changed after I graduated from college, when I moved west and started guiding bird hunters in central Montana. Each day, my clients and I followed my dogs over the prairies east of Great Falls in search of wild sharptail grouse, Hungarian partridge, or pheasant. The job offered the best "office" imaginable, but it also produced moments that forced me to look at upland bird hunting through a new lens.

I remember the first time I had a young dog bump a covey of birds instead of holding point. I went through the necessary corrections and training before letting the pup return to hunting. As we continued across the field, one of my clients asked about the "art" of training pointing dogs. For the next ten minutes, I stumbled through an attempt to

articulate my approach with young dogs. I tried to explain the techniques I had observed from my favorite dog handlers over the years—the ones that best instilled in the pup a balance of confidence, accountability, and a little enthusiastic risk taking. When I finished, the hunters nodded and smiled, seemingly entertained but not fully understanding. We continued on our hunt and I thought more about my answer, reflecting more on the philosophies of dog training, and playing with the best ways to put these intuitions into words.

I remember the first time I watched a hunter become completely rattled from the explosive covey rise of wild Hungarian partridge. Throughout the rest of the morning, he walked into every point tense with excitement and anticipation, and missed on every shot he fired. I watched him struggle with feeling both exhilarated and frustrated at the same time. Toward the end of the morning's hunt, we stopped at the top of a hill, watered the dogs, and sat as we looked at the native grasslands and mountains around us. He told me he couldn't remember shooting so poorly before in his life. We took turns describing the thrill and emotions that flood a person's senses during a wild bird flush. We talked about how time becomes convoluted in the intensity of the moment, causing a hunter to hurry a shot or not properly mount the gun. We celebrated the chaos of the moment, talking through the experience step by step—something I had not done before. When we finished, we stood and he exhaled deeply before we started back toward the truck. He didn't miss a bird all afternoon.

My seven years as a guide produced endless amounts of similar moments that allowed me to explore upland bird hunting through other people and their experiences. I got to watch hunters marvel at their first sharptail grouse, describe to them its legacy as a native species in the wild Montana landscape, and show them the makeup of its crop, which often included western stoneseed—a rock-hard kernel from a plant whose roots were used by local Native Americans as a natural contraceptive. On days when clients brought their own retrievers, I would leave my black Lab behind at the lodge, and would return in the evening to find out she had stayed perched on top of the dog trailer all day, staring straight ahead, not moving an inch until she saw my truck come back up the driveway. I got to guide a group of women for several years and watched them interact with upland hunting in ways that challenged the old, conventional, male-centric approaches to the sport.

After having been around wingshooting my entire life, I found myself encountering new moments that gave me pause and produced feelings of excitement and humility. These moments allowed me to appreciate upland hunting to an extent that had been subconscious during my childhood. It also introduced me to many people and their unique pathways through the sport.

This past fall, my wife and I started bringing our two-year-old daughter along on upland hunts. While one of us handled the dogs and walked in on points, the other would carry our daughter in the backpack, keeping her at a safe distance but also letting her take it all in. She would frequently ask to get down and walk for part of the hunt, help hold the water bottles when the dogs would come in for a drink, and pet the feathers of the birds that we shot before we placed them in the back of our vests. She would echo our calls to the dogs and yell "Boom" when someone shot at a covey rise. I would smile the entire time, watching her soak it up and take it all for granted, just like I did when I was a kid. At the end of the hunt, we would load her into her car seat and ask if she had fun. "Yeah!" she would say, raising her eyebrows. I would pull out on the county road and glance at her in the rearview mirror, knowing it wouldn't be long before she was finding her own path through upland hunting, helping to evolve the sport and helping me and other old-timers define and articulate why upland hunting is so special.

# Introduction

by REID BRYANT

There is something essentially beautiful about upland bird hunting. I have always known this. I can tell you now that the beauty comes from wide spaces, and slanting autumn sunlight, and a dog transfixed by a cone of scent. Something opens deep in your heart when a feathered wedge of the landscape breaks free and thunders skyward, and you see it framed against a sliver of the season, until it becomes all you see. Regardless of your philosophical leanings, or your thoughts on the joys or evils of meat, there is something elemental and honest about committing so wholly to a task that you suspend a piece of motion and watch it tumble to the ground, while feathers fall like thistledown. The weight of a bird still warm in your hand feels like a treasure, and a full game bag feels like all the riches of Araby.

The irony is that I understood these things long before I'd seen them, or felt them, or tasted them. I loved upland hunting before I ever picked up a gun, or heard the whirr of a flushing bird, or walked into the tangled corners of my native New England with intention. I cannot explain how, but from the time I was a little boy, I knew that bird hunting spoke to me in an acutely personal way. It called to me from a place deeper than my experience, which was starched and suburban and void of bloodstained feathers. But somewhere in my bones I could feel the pull of the uplands. I could picture myself, even as a young child, following a dog through the Octobers of my life, wielding a shotgun to great effect, and becoming a master of something rich in tradition, and richer still in that essential poetry.

Despite my romantic ideals, there was a very real and not insignificant hurdle that rose before me. I grew up on the outskirts of Boston, Massachusetts, in a family that neither approved of hunting nor willingly leaned in to the perceived savagery of killing things. Guns were inherently harmful and not allowed, and though my father had been given a .22 on his twelfth birthday, my mother made sure that my boyhood shooting was the quieter sort, achieved with pantomimed shotguns aimed at robins and crows. I felt silly about this even then, but in my day to day, this was hunting, or as near as I could see getting to it. I'd linger over the images of upland gunners that graced the pages of Orvis catalogs, and assume that those plaid-wearing and pipe-smoking folks had simply been granted

upbringings more fortunate than mine. After all, my dog-eared copies of *Field & Stream* were chock full of storybook boys who'd been ushered gingerly but sternly into the uplands by benevolent fathers and grandfathers. Those boys were given first bird dog pups. Those boys unwrapped sixteen-gauge shotguns on Christmas morning. Those boys learned hard lessons about responsibility by being given *real* responsibility and the license to do big and irreversible things. In each case, the uplands were the classroom, guns and birds the algorithmic variables, and elder relatives the professors. Those boys spent weekends chasing pheasant and grouse and quail while I spent my weekends chasing soccer balls, and wishing for a mentor with a spaniel and a gun. Alas, it just wasn't to be.

Wonderfully, the things that live within our souls eventually, invariably, see the light of day. I dated a girl in high school whose best friend's father turned out to be a bird hunter. He kept a setter and a German shorthaired pointer in a backyard kennel, and shot birds each Saturday. He was, needless to say, a bit of an anomaly in our neck of the woods. Every Sunday, after his return from church, he'd clean his game and clean his guns, and he'd suffer the incessant questions of his daughter's best friend's boyfriend. It was with him, at his basement workbench, that I first smelled Hoppe's Number 9 powder solvent, and first held a dead game bird in my hands. It was with him that I learned a shotgun has a wonderful weight, a lively heaviness that is full of possibility. It was in his study that I was offered my first German beer, and taught that a true gentleman has at least two dogs and at least three guns, a qualification I've tried to maintain ever since. I asked this man repeatedly to take me along, to let me follow him on one of his forays. He was patient with me, but dodged my requests in the way that stately older men do, steering the conversation away from my joining him and into other business. Always there was that ambiguous time frame of "some point later in the fall," and

I was young enough and hopeful enough to wait. But the day never came, and I broke up with the girl, and promises drifted off into the forgotten corners where they gather dust.

After a not-insignificant period of contemplation that perplexed my parents no end, I enrolled in a small college in northern Vermont, in a village where, I like to say, hunting was as much a piece of the social fabric as the town meeting. Among my professors were men who saw in me an honest desire to learn, or at the very least a relentless curiosity about bird hunting. These were the men I'd longed for in my childhood; bearded and bedecked in wool plaid, they exhaled the woods-wisdom that I so desperately wanted. They smoked pipes and smelled a little of evergreen pitch, and in fall there always seemed to be a freckled dog in their truck cabs. As time went by, they patiently welcomed me into the fold, and opened the door to something lovely: they allowed me to follow them into the field in autumn. I tromped along behind them, myself a man in the role of a tagalong boy, and I hit the deck when birds got up, and my teachers swung through and shot. I followed them into the gravel pit just off the hilltop Common, and pulled the trigger for the very first time on a by-god shotgun. They watched amused as I missed my first 100 clay targets. They fed me my first game dinners. They let me touch the unblinking eye of a beautiful bird from which life had just departed.

With the proximity of all of these experiences, I sewed up the remaining prerequisites: I sat through a summertime hunter's safety course alongside the local grade-school kids and proudly received a passing mark. I purchased my first hunting license, and acquired a wobbly side-by-side twelve gauge and oiled it lovingly. On the last September Saturday of my twenty-first year, I drove to the little piece of conifer woods just south of Little Hosmer Pond, and I slipped two shells into the gun. I walked out into a resplendent autumn full of purpose, and somehow in that moment I

found the bit of myself that I'd been looking for all along. A ruffed grouse got up a good distance away, right on the field edge, and I fired both barrels with no hope of possibly hitting. I opened the gun and looked sheepishly over my shoulder, waiting for a reprimand from that hidden authority that had kept hunting so long beyond my reach. And wouldn't you know it? All I saw was a hillside of turning maples and a twisting gravel road. I looked back toward the field edge and smiled. This, all of this, was finally sanctioned, and no heavy hand was ever to descend that would keep me from trudging deeper into the thick of it.

I had become an upland bird hunter.

Now, there were days and weeks to come before a first bird fell, months and years before a first bird dog shared my bed, and decades before I found myself in a career that revolved directly around upland hunting. In that span of time I walked miles in pursuit of birds and burned a heap of powder, and grew increasingly in love with the poetry that had been plain to me in boyhood. All the while, I contemplated the journey, and wished that the few years I'd lost to not hunting could be mine once more. If only that "country uncle," with all the pipe smoke and woods-wisdom, could have been available to me so much sooner. If only, if only . . .

So here I am, in the first blush of middle age, in a position to create some semblance of that "country uncle," if only in words and images. It is my sincere hope that this book serves to expedite the journey that I wallowed through, making it slightly less painful, and slightly more linear, for aspiring hunters. If, like me, you have felt that the gulf between you and the world of upland hunting is wide and deep, I hope this book will help you: the gulf may be wide, and it may be deep, but it is eminently crossable. You, like me, can become an upland hunter. You can paint yourself into that image of guns and dogs and autumn days. You can give yourself a lifetime of Octobers. So, too, if you are looking to redefine some of your thoughts about upland hunting, let this book serve as a point of reference. And if you are simply looking for a collection of lovely photos, and some ramblings scribbled down by a dreamy-eyed bird shooter, then you are among friends. Brian and I are grateful for the chance to walk beside you through all facets of upland bird hunting while expressing our relationship to the sport through authentic photography from the field and a good dose of personal anecdote. This story, and these lessons, are our lessons too; we look forward to sharing the magic and majesty of upland bird hunting with each of you.

The What and the Why

Chapter 1

The What and the Why

This book deals exclusively with upland bird hunting. This clarification is important right off the bat, for upland bird hunting is unique, both with regard to tactics and intended quarry. Upland bird hunting, or upland hunting as I'll largely refer to it, will be defined thus: the act of hunting upland game birds (i.e., grouse, pheasant, partridge, etc.) with a shotgun, often in the company of a purpose-specific gun dog.

There are several components to this definition. Under a greater degree of magnification, let's assume the following:

■ Upland game birds are edible species of birds that do not spend appreciable periods of time in or on the water (that is to say, they are not waterfowl). They are chiefly species of the order *Galliformes*, which is composed of heavy-bodied, chicken-like birds. The legal pursuit of these species is sanctioned, in North America anyway, by state, provincial, or federal law.

■ A shotgun is a firearm designed to propel a number of small metal pellets called shot. A shotgun is loaded with shotshells, which come in a variety of shapes and sizes.

■ A purpose-specific gun dog is a dog trained to locate, point, flush (i.e., make fly), or retrieve game.

These are the defining elements of upland hunting. But these definitions leave several gaps concerning the intricacies of the actual process. "Where do you find upland birds?" the aspiring hunter might ask. "What kind of shotgun do I need to use?" "What sort of dog points birds, and what sort flushes them?"

All of these questions, and several more, are soon to be examined in depth.

Ironically, just a few generations ago, the majority of folks in North America knew the answers to the aforementioned questions. As the populace of this continent has grown, and the food structure of our culture has made meat relatively inexpensive and widely available, upland hunting has shriveled into a shadow of its former self. What used to be a part of our common language has become generally obsolete, and what used to be a practical and acceptable means of harvesting table fare has become anomalous, and to many, somewhat unthinkable. Guns have taken on a wildly different role in contemporary culture, as has their possession and use. The liability potential of welcoming strangers onto private land has made "No Trespassing" signs ubiquitous throughout rural America. With all of these factors added to an increasingly dense and urbanized way of living, it is no wonder that upland hunting has been lost to so many.

I am willing to bet that our great-grandfathers knew how to safely handle a shotgun. I'm willing to bet that our great-grandmothers at some point ate a wild piece of meat, even if it was served in a big-city restaurant. I'm willing to bet that all of these folks had either seen or taken part in the processing of a dead bird, chicken or otherwise. I'm willing to bet that they all knew what a shotgun shell looked

like, and, at some point, cleaned feathers from the kitchen sink.

But change, and rapid change especially, has removed upland hunting from our common dialect and our common practice. So too has change moved us away from an experiential world into a largely virtual one. We are indoors more than we've ever been, and we are increasingly removed from our natural surroundings. We produce in quantity and dispose in quantity, and make our material decisions with an eye toward obsolescence. Our amusement more and more revolves around a fabricated experience that we've designed for the sole purpose of entertaining us. Our food has become synthesized and shrink-wrapped, and it leaves very little honest substance to linger on our tongues, or in our souls. I feel grateful, however, and optimistic that current generations are pushing back against these cultural, environmental, and dietary trends. The past decade has seen an incredible rise in the focus on locally sourced food, protected open lands, and experiential learning. It is somehow as though the generation most entrenched in a synthetic culture is identifying the need for something deeper, something more time honored. Folks who spend their days building digital communities or trading commodities over abstract channels are finding, with regard to their leisure time, the need for tactile engagement in something that aligns and engages the senses. People are finding value in poignant and pointed entrée into the natural world. They want to enter the landscape, to source their food from that same landscape, and to follow it lovingly all the way to the table. Our culture is looking to remember what it means to be human. Hunting becomes a logical venue for meeting these needs. The only problem, for many anyway, is where and how to begin.

There are many opportunities to learn how to shoot. For those interested in wingshooting (i.e., shooting flying targets with a shotgun), games such as trap, skeet, and sporting clays provide a wonderful outlet. Learning to shoot is not difficult; learning to shoot successfully takes time and practice, but the actual opportunity of learning how to handle a shotgun is fairly available. Classes and clinics abound at regional gun clubs, and state fish and wildlife agencies are keen to make shooting instruction available to aspiring sportsmen. Learning the proper and safe use of a shotgun is a vital component of a hunter's progress, and it should neither be overlooked nor taken lightly. But shooting is not hunting, and wingshooting is not upland hunting. Hunting is a distinctly different beast, and from the very start, before any bird has been shot or killed or cleaned, it requires a wider skill set and a wider understanding.

The demystification of upland hunting hinges on one central point: upland hunting is, like all hunting, undeniably real. It bloodies the hands, and, when done to success, it removes a little piece of something lovely from the living community. It is also, like life itself, a dynamic and inherently unpredictable endeavor. Part of what draws people into the hunt, and part of what makes a bird in the hand so special, is that a whole range of circumstances result in the collision of lead and wingbeats that leads to a bird in the oven. But by learning how to prepare for the field, by learning about guns and gauges, by learning about habitat, and by learning to identify our resident game birds, we come infinitely closer to something elementally connected and therefore elementally human. When we learn safe gun handling and field etiquette, we ensure our safe and welcome return to the field. All of this learning, and all of this practice, will heighten our chances for success. An aspiring hunter, armed solely with intention, is in a perfect position to embark on this learning process. In fact, an aspiring hunter, armed with knowledge and intention, is an aspiring hunter no more; he or she is a hunter, an upland hunter plain and simple.

And it goes without saying that an upland hunter is, to my way of thinking anyway, a wonderful thing to be.

A Brief History

 Chapter 2

A Brief History

In the infancy of my own experience, I looked back, way back, into the almanac of a hunting tradition. This framed my longing, and charted a course for my future. The upland hunting we aspire to incorporates modern techniques and modern weaponry, but the tradition of the hunt, particularly in North America, wends its way deep into the annals of our history.

Prior to the colonization of North America, the landscape was thick with native upland birds.

Aside from the endemic species that continue to inhabit the North American uplands, the indigenous people of this continent bore witness to several species that no longer grace our fields or forests. No doubt this abundance of winged game was a mainstay of the Pre-Columbian diet, and it was taken by numerous methods. Remember, however, that food and feathers were the desired result, and sport was a frivolity that our first bird hunters had no time for. Snaring, noosing, trapping, and indeed shooting were standard means of winged game getting, and no doubt the native hunters were adept at the task. But it would take the arrival of European colonists to shift what had been a subsistence effort into something slightly different.

The first people to hunt North American game birds with modern methods (guns) were British and European colonists, whose arrival in the New World in the late sixteenth century initiated our modern hunting heritage. As with the Native American hunter, however, this hunting heritage was less driven by sport and more by opportunism.

The colonists faced the massive undertaking of feeding themselves, and doing so in a land that did not take kindly to European agricultural practices. With landfall, the colonists of Massachusetts and Virginia faced several years' worth of land clearing, shelter building, and fuel gathering before they might effectively put any contemporary farming practices in place. In order to survive, therefore, they made great use of the available game stocks. Chief among these species, with regard to birds anyway, were the heath hen, ruffed grouse, bobwhite quail, and passenger pigeon, along with various and sundry waterfowl, which presented such an abundant and easily obtained food resource that they made regular appearances on colonial tables. Unfortunately, several of these species also fell prey to overhunting in short order. Remarkable as it may seem, it took little more than the proverbial blink of an eye for an overzealous hunting culture to push the heath hen and passenger pigeon to extinction. Now, for fear that this treatise become a forum for finger wagging, I'll not wax too poetic on our responsibility

as hunters to preserve the stocks of huntable upland game birds. Instead, let's consider those colonists, and how their enthusiasm for the hunt might be somewhat similar to the one we feel today.

Many if not most of our early settlers came from the British Isles or mainland Europe. No doubt there was a rich hunting culture in those places too, but much of the land, and indeed much of the game upon it, belonged to the nobility. Generally speaking, the common man or woman had neither the access to firearms nor the legal go-ahead to shoot game, flying game especially. But sport was of little consequence to the colonial settler. These folks were far more interested in survival, and the prevalence of game in the New World made survival and westward expansion possible. Game was taken by whatever means necessary, and though guns were used, there was little concern for "sport." A ready food source, a common wealth, was leaping and crawling and flying and swimming all over North America, and the European settlers made good use of it.

As time passed, these settlers came to harvest game for both food and profit, by shooting and trapping in the most efficient means possible. Guns capable of shooting a hailstorm of projectiles were used to harvest upland game en masse, usually as the birds ran, sat, or roosted. Though these firearms were efficient killing machines, they were far from dynamic in design; cumbersome, heavy, and ruefully hard to discharge, these same firearms made effective wingshooting a futile endeavor. The very idea of choosing to shoot an isolated bird on the wing was antithetical to the survival spirit of the era, and would have been laughable, or downright wasteful. It would take the next couple of centuries, and the steady refinement of the modern shotgun, before shooting flying gained ground as a sport, and the shooting of birds in flight became a favored means of taking game.

Through the eighteenth century, bird shooting on the large estates of the British Isles rose in popularity. As was the custom, wealthy nobles were thrilled to indulge in excess, and game—posing a

challenge rather than a survival necessity—was shot on the wing or on the run. By the mid-nineteenth century, the breech-loader was taking a form and degree of performance recognizable to the contemporary shooters of today. The overarching culture of landed gentry, however, retained the most desirable game birds (i.e., introduced pheasant, grouse, partridge, and ducks) on the larger estates. The common thinking was that game belonged to the owner of the land on which it was taken, and land was a commodity passed down through bloodlines. Clearly, the wealthy owned most of the game. Poaching became an art form, though not a sporting endeavor, and bird shooting took on an identity as a sport of privilege and exclusivity. Hence, when the populace of the new United States separated dramatically from England, the conventional understanding of game laws were jettisoned too, in honor of a more democratic attitude.

Stateside, matters evolved in response. In the early days of America, birds continued to be shot, caught, killed, and eaten as a part of our common wealth. Though game was abundant, the newly independent country was both expanding and filling up quickly. By 1770, game stocks within the metropolitan areas were noticeably diminished, and twelve of the thirteen colonies established closed seasons. The increasing scarcity of game generated a commercial demand for it, and market hunters, seeing a window of opportunity, ventured further afield to return birds to the city markets, in turn pressuring stocks all the more. This increasing scarcity brought the colonists full circle, and not long after the Revolution, and the conscious dismissal of old-world tradition, American landowners began to enforce trespassing laws. In 1790, Hungarian partridge were the first nonnative game bird species introduced to the New World, on a private property in New Jersey. This act punctuated the realization that game stocks could be supplemented by nonnative species, and initiated an era of North American hunting that considered the shooting of birds on the wing a sport worthy of cultivation and manipulation. The rest, you might say, is history.

The 1850s saw the arrival of modern, breech-loading shotguns in America, and the downturn of the muzzle-loader. Ammunition quickly became more efficient, and westward expansion offered new avenues for the adventurous upland hunter. The marriage of rail lines and refrigerated train cars enabled western market hunters and their correlative impact to seep west to the Pacific, answering a demand for game meat that was to prove unsustainable. By the late 1800s, market hunting was banned in America, the pheasant was gaining ground as an introduced species, and modern shotguns were being designed, built, and sold domestically. What was borne of a sporting tradition had come full circle, venturing through a period of grim necessity, then market-driven opportunity, to bloom into what the shooting of game birds on the wing resembles today: a true sport.

Currently, there are opportunities for upland hunting in all fifty states. This hunting runs the gamut from the pursuit of indigenous bird species on public land to highly managed, pay-to-play opportunities for farm-raised and nonnative birds, often at a high price. Regardless of format, however, upland hunting clings on as a part of a rich, if often overlooked, sporting tradition.

What We Are After

Chapter 3

What We Are After

Intention is a critical primary weapon in the hunter's quiver. Deciding to hunt upland birds is the psychological impetus for all that follows, and the first step on a wonderful journey. But once that intention is clear, realities fill the frame. The very first of these realities requires that hunters understand the birds, their habits, and the environments they prefer.

Upland game birds are defined as such less by taxonomy and more by general habit, and, to be quite honest, palatability. Writer Stephen Bodio, in his wonderful essay titled "Meat," declaims that all (or at least most) birds can be wonderful to eat. I don't doubt that this is true, but generations, indeed millennia, of trial and error have led us to a handful of species that are particularly prized as table fare. Largely, though not exclusively, these are ground-nesting, chicken-like birds. They exhibit a plump, meaty breast, and powerful but sinewy legs and wings. They spend the bulk of their time foraging on the ground, and their preferred means of escape, after running, is an eruption into flight known as a flush. These birds, in North America anyway, range in size from the diminutive American woodcock, which hovers around four ounces, to the transplanted Himalayan snowcock, which can tip

Grouse

The North American grouses are the continent's preeminent native game birds. They fall under the subfamily *Tetraoninae*, and are collected into several distinct species. These species include the spruce grouse; blue (dusky/sooty) grouse; willow, rock, and white-tailed ptarmigan; ruffed grouse; sage grouse; Gunnison (sage) grouse; sharp-tailed grouse; and greater and lesser prairie chicken. These birds have a wide dispersal across North America, and frequent a range of habitats. The grouses are wild in the purest sense, and have universally resisted domestication. They are distinguished from their cousins the partridges by small feathers in the nostrils and legs feathered to the toes. Differing species inhabit woodlands and grasslands from the subarctic to the high plains desert. The North American grouses are wild game birds emblematic of the unrestrained and undeveloped country still extant in parts of the continent.

Grouses are remarkably adaptable. They are specifically denominated as chionophiles, meaning that evolution has provided them with physical adaptations that make them able to resist harsh, wintry conditions. They universally develop pectinations in winter, or comblike structures on the toes that serve to distribute weight and allow mobility over the snow surface. They have a distinctly

the scales upward of six pounds. They are virtually all associated within the order of *Galliformes*, which describes heavy-bodied, ground-dwelling birds with short, powerful bills. They are chiefly omnivorous, with diets that lean heavily on mast and vegetation, complemented by invertebrates and insects as opportunity allows. There are, of course, anomalies. The American woodcock bucks many of the descriptors of the common game birds, but that too will become clear in short order.

In North America different species of upland game birds occupy different regions and different ecosystem cover types. For this reason, each is hunted slightly differently, though the general rules of hunting remain consistent. A desert quail hunter in southern Arizona will no doubt tread a far different landscape than an Alaskan ptarmigan hunter, but similar dogs, similar guns, and similar safety measures will bring these widely different species to bag. The greatest difference is in identification, and in the birds themselves and their corresponding habitat.

For the sake of the learning process, we'll begin with an overview of the game birds of North America. Though not a definitive list, this covers the generalities. Included is information about requisite dogs, guns, and loads (types of shells and shot), though these details will be clarified more thoroughly in following chapters.

RUFFED GROUSE

varied diet, and an ability to avoid predation by roosting in varied pieces of the terrain. They have, in short, evolved in concert with our northern climes, and their ability to thrive in rugged environments is inspirational.

The grouses vary in behavior in response to habitat, and cover type often dictates how they are best hunted. That said, the majority are pursued equally well with either a flushing or pointing dog. As table fare, grouses vary from species to species. Spruce and sage grouse are known for meat flavored heavily by their namesake food sources, whereas ruffed grouse have a sweet white meat not dissimilar to lean chicken. Sharp-tailed grouse and ptarmigan meat is rich and dark in color, retaining a richer flavor nearly reminiscent of duck. All grouses, prepared properly, are prized on the plate.

Forest grouses can be successfully taken with a twenty- or even twenty-eight-gauge shotgun, but prairie and tundra birds require something bigger; many a sharptail has fallen to the sixteen- or twelve-gauge gun. Shot size for ruffed grouse in the New England woods can be as small as No. 8, but open-land grouse require No. 7.5 shot and moderate chokes for clean shooting. One famed New England shooter always loads his second barrel with No. 6 shot, thinking that the second, farther shot will require deep penetration at a distant bird. His sage opinion is that a hard-hitting single pellet is far better than a smattering of small shot that lacks killing power.

Pheasant

Common or ring-necked pheasants are perhaps the most widely recognized upland game birds in the world. They are highly sought after for the sport they present, as well as their quality as table fare. A cock pheasant is a large, beautiful, vibrant bird whose wild populations are universally supplemented by pen-raised or farmed specimens.

RING-NECKED PHEASANT

Ironically, though pheasants may be the iconic game bird of North America, they are a non-native species. With origins in China and East Asia, pheasants have been introduced around the world, with initial North American stocking taking place in Oregon's Willamette Valley in 1881. This initial stocking was accomplished by then US Consul (to China) Owen Nickerson Denny, who could only have guessed at the future of pheasants in North America. Wild reproduction of pheasants took off successfully throughout agricultural regions, and state stockings of these birds have maintained them as a game species throughout that range. Hybrids

and melanistic mutations of the common pheasant are sometimes seen, but by and large these birds appear in typical form throughout farmlands, wetland edges, and grain-rich regions of North America. They are the most commonly used game bird for preserve-style and driven hunts.

Wild or assimilated pheasants have a tendency to run in thin cover. They often sneak ahead of advancing hunters, and can prove challenging for a pointing dog to pin. In most areas, gaudily colored cock birds are legally taken while hens are protected. If the ornamentation of the cock pheasant were not enough to set it apart in flight, males also cackle loudly when flushing. Their long tail feathers create a large silhouette, a feature that, along with the boisterous flush, can make for a challenging target in that there is an awful lot of commotion to make sense of. In many areas, flushing dogs such as Labs and springer spaniels are preferred for hard-running pheasants, though pen-raised cock birds and hens can hold well for a pointing dog.

Owing to their predilection for grain, pheasants make a beloved game meat for the home kitchen. Their flavor varies a bit based on diet, but the substantial breast is white meat resembling lean chicken. The legs are edible but sinewy, and must be prepared accordingly; stewing or braising is the preferred method.

Pheasants are best taken with a moderately choked twelve- or sixteen-gauge gun, filled with No. 6 shot.

Partridge

Though genetically similar to our native grouses, our partridges are Eurasian transplants that include the gray or Hungarian partridge, the chukar partridge, and the Himalayan snowcock. The gray partridge or Hun is a cherished "wild" game bird of the North American uplands, with the

CHUKAR PARTRIDGE

largest populations occurring through the Grain Belt of the upper Midwest and Mountain West. Huns prefer cool and dry grasslands and cultivated grain fields, and they have a noted predilection for wheat as a food source. Despite the name, Huns are decidedly more rusty brown than gray, and females are slightly paler in coloration than males and lack their distinctive mahogany chest patch. They tend to be found in groups or coveys, and once dispersed will recall the covey with a series of scratchy "kut-kut-kut" vocalizations.

Slightly larger than the Hun, and far more identifiable, is the chukar partridge. Chukars in North America were transplanted from their native Eurasian range, with initial US stocks arriving from Afghanistan and Nepal. The chukar has been widely introduced to rocky, semiarid regions across the globe, and is a common game bird of preserves and stocked hunting grounds. In the wild, these birds exist primarily in the rocky hill country of the American West, where they form coveys of ten or more individuals. They are brownish varying to distinct gray across the back and breast, with characteristic black barring on the flanks and a striking black mask, or gorget, over the eyes. Chukars, like their nearest cousins the rock partridge and red-legged partridge, have featherless red legs. In typical cover, they prefer to flush downhill and run up. Hunters in chukar country should be prepared to wear out some boot leather.

The Himalayan snowcock is also a transplant from the Eurasian high country, and isolated populations of US birds occur in the Ruby Mountains of Nevada. Few North American hunters pursue snowcocks, and those who do rarely take them on the wing. That said, they can be hunted over dogs, and powerful, hard-going Labs are likely the best choice.

Partridges are hunted well over pointers and flushers, though in the case of chukars a steady retrieving dog can be essential. Steep and deep terrain requires a dog that will return shot birds to hand. Flushes occur downhill and into canyons, so retrieves can be both tiresome and treacherous. That said, most partridges hold well for a pointing dog.

Partridge meat is delicious and copious. As foragers, partridges tend to exist on grains, seeds, and insects, and their meat is light in color and moderately rich. The breast meat is white, the legs and thighs slightly darker.

Partridges can be taken with twenty-gauge guns and larger, but in open country, a twelve gauge can be a godsend. That said, partridges require some walking, so choose your gun wisely with regard to weight. No. 7.5 and No. 6 shot should suffice, though snowcocks necessitate something larger. Moderate to open chokes should work well on these fast-flushing birds.

Quail

Among North America's most recognizable native game birds are quails, with the northern bobwhite quail being the most familiar. Beloved for their namesake call, bobwhites were once widely distributed through the grasslands and pine forests of the East. They are the only small *Galliforme* native to this region, and have seen a rapid decline in recent years due to changing agricultural and land-use practices and the growing dispersal of nonnative fire ants. Bobwhites are, like all quails, ground-dwelling, coveying birds with a strong communal instinct. When properly conditioned, their flush is explosive and startling; they are commonly pen raised and released for the purpose of preserve-style upland hunting.

The other quails are similarly smallish game birds primarily found in the mountains and deserts of the American West. These include the California (valley), mountain, Gambel's, scaled (blue), and Mearns (Montezuma) quails. All of these birds form ground-dwelling groups or coveys. Each has a particular range and habitat, with some overlap occurring between species. Gambel's, valley, and mountain quails each show a distinctive plume or topknot that makes them readily identifiable.

Quails are hunted most frequently over pointing dogs, though their tendency to hold tight in thick cover makes an accompanying flushing dog a benefit. English cockers have become a beloved companion of dedicated quail hunters, as they will put coveys of pointed birds into rapid flight once two or more pointers have the covey pinned. Increasingly, cockers are finding favor on the storied quail plantations of the southeastern United States.

Quails prove excellent on the plate. They are small and delicate in flavor, composed of ample white meat. They are thin skinned as well, and despite their rapid initial flush or covey rise, they are killed at relatively close range. Twenty- and twenty-eight-gauge guns perform well on quails, and some shooters even swear by the diminutive .410. Shot sizes No. 7.5 to No. 9 are adequate, and open chokes are preferred.

Woodcock

Beloved in its range, the American woodcock also goes by a host of colloquial pseudonyms, namely timberdoodle, mud bat, and bogsucker. It is a quirky little bird, designated officially as a shorebird, but found in moist uplands across eastern North America. The American woodcock migrates extensively with the changing season, spending winter months as far south as Louisiana and summer nesting months deep into the Canadian

BOBWHITE QUAIL

AMERICAN WOODCOCK

Maritimes. Migration occurs largely at night, and groups or flights of woodcocks will descend upon a piece of cover seemingly out of the blue during migration. The woodcock's diet consists almost exclusively of invertebrates and earthworms, probed from the soil with a distinctively long, prehensile bill.

The woodcock is unmistakable in the uplands, though it does resemble the common snipe, which prefers marshy wetlands. Small in size, these birds have a mottled black and brown plumage that makes them almost invisible within their native habitat. The bill is nearly as long as the entire body, and large eyes are positioned high on the head for maximum range of visibility. This remarkable visual capability enables an awareness of threats while the bird plunges its bill into the soil in search of food. Due to habitat loss, woodcock numbers have been in steady decline since the 1960s. In the North, they are often found in conjunction with ruffed grouse, whose habitat needs are similar.

From the palatability standpoint, woodcock meat is like Dr. Pepper: you either love it or hate it. The small breast is dark and livery in flavor, with a rich and earthy undertone. The legs of the woodcock are, ironically, the only white meat on the bird. Historically, the entrails of the woodcock are prepared inside the cavity and the head remains intact, with the long bill piercing the thighs. The cooked intestine or trail can be served alongside the heart and liver on a toast round, and the brain too can be eaten by the gastronomically adventuresome. In many parts of Europe, where the collective palate has not been diluted, woodcocks are considered among the most prized of all winged game.

Being a small, thin-skinned bird, woodcocks do not need much killing. If hunted exclusively, a twenty-eight gauge with open chokes is more than ample, loaded with No. 9 shot. If hunted alongside grouse, beware that a close-quarters encounter with large shot and tight chokes can devastate a woodcock and turn a beautiful bird into a palm full of livery pulp.

Doves

Though not hunted in a traditional "upland" sense, namely over pointing or flushing dogs, doves are a longstanding favorite of the North American game birds. Doves are typically hunted by pass-shooting—that is to say, shot as they fly to and from the roost or as they descend onto agricultural fields. Doves exhibit a remarkable dexterity on the wing, and owing to flight speeds upward of forty miles per hour, they are highly regarded by wing-shooters. The most common and most hunted of the North American doves is the mourning dove, which has distribution throughout the United States and much of Canada.

MOURNING DOVE

Fast-flying doves require no particular dog work, and can be hunted from a sedentary position. Hidden on field edges, gunners swing through darting doves and miss at an alarming rate. Twelve-gauge guns on down to twenties are suitable, as is No. 7.5 shot. Dove breasts are quite small, but when stuffed with a pickled jalapeno, wrapped in bacon, and grilled until the bacon is crisp, they are a sublime afternoon meal.

In Summary

The prevalence of any aforementioned species depends almost entirely on location. The New England bird hunter will have access to ruffed grouse and woodcocks as common native wild birds, with a smattering of introduced pheasants and bobwhite quail on public lands. In the Southwest, desert quail will be the predominate species, with doves and potentially some pheasants thrown in. Shooting preserves across the continent tend to focus on an offering that includes pheasant, chukar partridge, and bobwhite quail. Himalayan snowcocks are found only among the high peaks of Nevada's Ruby Mountains. On shooting preserves, the triumvirate of pheasant, chukar, and bobwhite quail is by far the most common. All upland birds, regardless of species, are magnificent examples of nature's artistry.

Guns and Shooting

 Chapter 4

Guns and Shooting

I have always been fascinated by the artistry of shotguns. There is something about the marriage of walnut and blued steel that oozes romance, and I've been a starry-eyed enthusiast since well before I ever held a shotgun in my hands. That said, the actual use of a gun, and certainly the purchase of one, can be fraught with intimidation.

The underlying truth about guns, and the one that should not, cannot, ever be forgotten, is that guns are dangerous weapons. They may be fascinating, they may be beautiful, they may be in some circumstances phenomenally valuable, but they are *always* capable of great harm. Guns require the utmost respect and careful handling, both in the field and out.

I have been lucky in my career in the outdoor industry to have visited some remarkable shooting destinations. I have met legendary hunters, dog trainers, and guides, and I have spent wonderful moments with the most gifted of outdoor writers. It is amazing to me, therefore, that among this cast

of seasoned professionals so many stories of near misses, or non-misses, rise to the surface when the topic turns to guns. This is not to say that my friends are necessarily at fault, or that hunting is by nature a dangerous activity. It is simply to say that accidents can happen when guns enter the frame. If you hunt long enough, you will hear these sad and frightening stories too, and they will rightly sober you. You will hear of dogs shot in the field, of supposedly unloaded guns blowing holes in truck cabs, and of hunting partners who have returned from the field scarred by the lead from a partner's misdirected shot. Each of these stories is one too many. It is our responsibility as shooters to try to render them obsolete.

Guns should be handled confidently and to great effect, and they should be at once fascinating and lovely. But they should always be respected and treated with the absolute, utmost caution. I would highly recommend that aspiring shooters and hunters undergo some formal instruction in safe gun handling in a controlled environment. Such educational opportunities are generally available through local gun clubs, state fish and wildlife agencies, or local police departments. Furthermore, laws concerning legal gun ownership, use, and transport vary state to state, so be certain to research the local guidelines for your area.

Shotguns come in an array of configurations, but the underlying premise remains the same: shotguns are loaded with a cartridge or shell, within which is housed a contained amount of both highly explosive powder and metal, typically lead, pellets. An explosion occurs when the primer is impacted by a shotgun's firing pin, and this explosion propels the aforementioned lead pellets out of the barrel in the direction of the target. This spray of pellets flies in a cluster called a shot column or shot string, which, upon impact, creates a roughly circular dispersal that is known as a pattern or shot spread. The pellets are intended to coincide with a moving target. Shotguns are comprised of the following parts: barrel, action or receiver, and stock. Shotgun stocks are typically made of wood or synthetics, while barrels and actions are made of steel.

Ammunition

A shotgun is a tool designed to hurl little bits of metal at a moving object. An understanding of the little bits of metal, and the explosion that hurls them, is fundamental to understanding the tool

SHOTGUN SHELL DIAGRAM

RIM BRASS HEAD SHELL CASE

PRIMER GUNPOWDER WAD SHOT

that instigates the explosion, and is central to the upland hunting game.

A modern shotgun shell, also called a shotshell or cartridge, is measured in gauge, length, shot size, and powder charge. It is constructed of a brass base and a plastic cylinder in which the innards—namely the powder, shot, and wad—are contained. The plastic cylinder is crimped on the top to retain all of the innards, and to open freely when discharged and the resultant propulsion of the shot occurs.

GAUGE

Shotgun gauge refers to the diameter of the bore, or, more simply, the inside diameter of the barrel. The common gauges for upland hunting include—in descending order of size—twelve, sixteen, twenty, twenty-eight, and .410. The twelve-gauge gun is likely the most common shotgun in existence. It is versatile, practical, and appropriate for hunting virtually any species of North American upland game. But what does the "twelve" in twelve gauge refer to? The answer to this question is, in itself, a glimpse back into a bygone era.

Gauge refers to the weight of a solid ball of lead that might fit perfectly in the bore of a shotgun, expressed as the inverse of said ball's weight as a fraction of a pound. For example, the ball of lead that perfectly fills the bore of a twelve-gauge shotgun weighs $1/12$ of a pound. In turn, twelve of these lead balls add up to a pound in weight. The lead ball that fits perfectly in a twenty-gauge bore weighs $1/20$ of a pound, and twenty of these balls equate to a pound in weight. This somewhat obscure measuring system holds true all the way down to the diminutive .410, which is actually a measurement of caliber (i.e., a direct numerical measurement of bore diameter, expressed as .41 inches). Gauge measurements stem from the days of cannonballs, when an "eight-pound cannon" or "eight-pounder" fired a round ball weighing eight pounds.

Gauge has varying degrees of pertinence when it comes to hunting; it often requires a correlative look at the other specifics of a shotshell, namely length and shot size, to articulate the shell's appropriate use. A twelve-gauge gun, though often considered bigger than a twenty-eight gauge, need only be larger in bore diameter. A twelve-gauge gun can in fact be both lighter in the hand, less punishing from a recoil standpoint, and more suited for small and thin-skinned birds than its smaller cousin. That said, when comparing a twelve-gauge shell to a twenty-eight-gauge shell of equal length and shot size, the twelve will generally contain a greater number of pellets due to its greater diameter and therefore greater volume.

■ LENGTH

Length refers to just that, the overall length of the shotshell. A longer shell can contain more powder and shot than a shorter one, though I might note that more does not always mean better, especially where ballistic efficiency is concerned. As you will see later in this chapter, the shotshell seats inside the breech end of the barrel and is held for firing in a section of the barrel called the chamber. The chamber has a certain length that correlates to the length of shotshell it can accommodate. Many British guns were built with two-and-a-half-inch-long chambers. These guns can only be fired with two-and-a-half-inch-long shells, which are somewhat hard to find on American shelves. The most common shell length for upland hunting is two and three-quarters inches, though certain conditions call for the three-inch shell. These two shells are interchangeable in the same gun, provided that the chamber accommodates the longer of the two. Hence, you can shoot a two-and-three-quarters-inch shell from a gun with a three-inch chamber, but you can't shoot a three-inch shell from a gun with a two-and-three-quarters-inch chamber. Chamber length in modern guns is often stamped on the barrel, denoted in some variation of the phrase "two-and-three-quarters-inch and three-inch shells." When in doubt, if a shell doesn't seat fully into the chamber, don't push it; though you may be able to force the shell's hand, the far safer bet is to switch to shorter ammunition, and have a gunsmith measure the chambers.

■ SHOT SIZE

Shot size describes the actual size of the pellets that are discharged when the shotgun is fired. These pellets are assigned numerical or alphabetical sizes wherein the shot size decreases as the number increases. Practical upland bird shot (never, *ever*, refer to the stuff that kills birds or clays as buckshot) begins at No. 9 or 10 on the small end, descending to No. 4 on the large end. Though other sizes exist, they are inapplicable for upland game under most circumstances. Shot is made of lead, steel, or a nontoxic alloy. Steel is less energetically efficient than lead, but it poses less threat of environmental contamination. Alloys such as those of tungsten/iron or tin/bismuth perform similarly to lead from a ballistic standpoint (i.e., they retain a good deal of downrange energy), but are nontoxic. Unfortunately, shells filled with alloy shot are often prohibitively expensive.

■ POWDER CHARGE

Powder charge is the last, and to my mind the most alchemic, measure of a shotgun shell. I also find powder charge to be a challenge for simple minds such as mine to grasp. Powder charge refers to the amount of powder contained in a shotshell (modern guns use what is known as smokeless powder as opposed to black powder). The amount of powder in a given shell is sometimes, albeit archaically, expressed in drams equivalent (dr. eq.), but more frequently in grains (a denomination of weight, not volume). A factory shotshell is also typically afforded a measurement of foot per second (fps) of muzzle velocity as the pellets exit the barrel. Confusing, right?

Basically, for every size and shape of pellet, a shotgun shell can create an efficient or an inefficient killing pattern. An efficient pattern creates an even dispersal of pellets, maintains good downrange potency, and avoids generating so much pressure inside the barrel that the structural integrity is compromised. For this reason, a greater powder charge is not always warranted or desired. Fast pellets don't always mean good patterns or shooting comfort. In general, factory loads designated for "game" or "target" use are sufficient for most upland hunting—and most target shooting for that matter—that you'll encounter.

■ OTHER TERMS

The only other bits and pieces of nomenclature regarding shotshells are brass, primer, and wad. The brass refers to the metal base of the standard shell. Some shooters refer to high-brass or low-brass shells. In simple terms, a high-brass shell often contains a greater powder charge and a bit more "oomph." The primer is the circular insert centered in the base of the shell. A primer contains a small bit of explosive material that, when struck by the firing pin, ignites the powder charge, in turn firing the gun; more on the mechanics of this process will follow in due course. The wad, in modern ammunition, is a barrier that serves two purposes. First, it separates the powder from the shot, maintaining the propulsion medium behind the projectiles. Second, it creates a seal between the powder and the shot that enables the explosive effect of the ignited powder to propel the shot out as a unit, rather than simply pushing the released pressure through the collection of pellets.

Anatomy of a Shotgun

■ BARRELS

Shotguns for upland hunting possess either one or two barrels (though in rare cases as many as four can be found on the same gun). The end of the barrel from which the shot exits is known as the muzzle. The muzzle of a shotgun barrel is assigned a constriction or choke based on how rapidly and to what degree the pellets are intended to disperse. The constriction occurs on the inside of the barrel, which, as noted, is known as the bore.

A shotgun barrel is basically a big cylinder with a fat end and a skinny end. Working back from the muzzle (skinny) end, we have some degree of constriction (i.e., choke), which gives way to the internal surface of the barrel (i.e., bore). Jumping to the end of the barrel opposite the muzzle, a shooter deposits shells into the breech end of the barrel, specifically into a recess called the chamber. The chamber is a two- to three-and-a-half-inch segment of the breech portion of the barrel that is slightly larger in diameter than the bore, specifically designed to hold a shotshell. Moving toward the muzzle, the chamber constricts to the bore diameter, and the transition area between the chamber and the bore is called the forcing cone.

Speaking in *very* simplistic terms, a standard twelve-gauge upland bird shell might spit out a few hundred lead pellets. As mentioned, pellets in flight occupy a three-dimensional space called a shot column, which gets bigger (i.e., spreads) with time

GUNS AND SHOOTING ■ 63

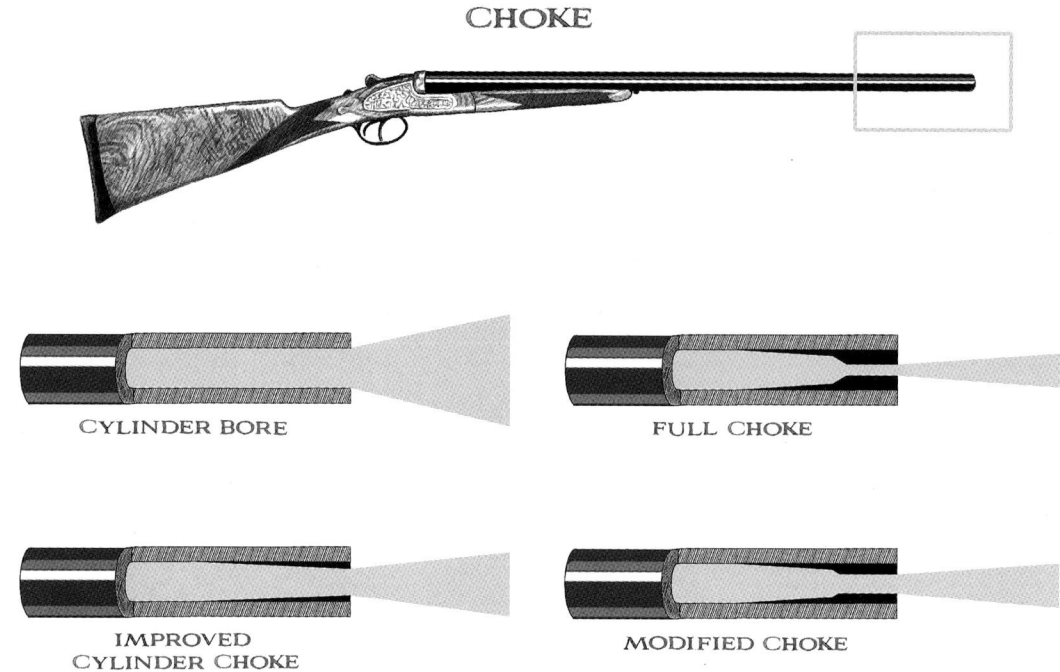

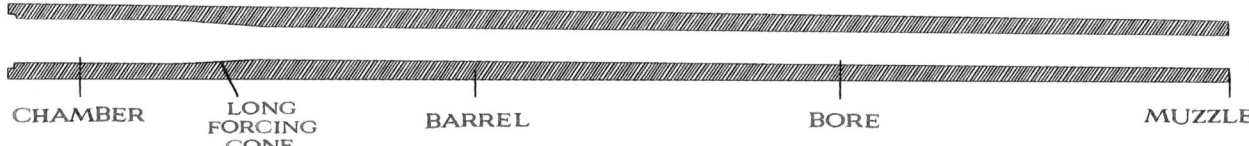

and distance. If this swarm of pellets were to hit a barn wall, the resulting impact would show up as a roughly circular, two-dimensional cluster of tiny holes, each representing the place where a piece of shot hit the wall. The cluster of holes in total would represent a dispersal of pellets that is known as a pattern or shot spread. If a bird had been glued to the same barn wall, in the same space that the pattern chose to occupy, the bird too would exhibit lots of little holes. Add dynamic movement, subtract the barn wall and glue, and this is how birds are shot on the wing.

Choke determines how dense or how open that pattern winds up being, and it can prove a challenging concept to grasp, as it hinges upon physical forces that occur within the barrel. Physically, a choke is just as it sounds: a gradual constriction of the barrel over the terminal two to three inches that end in the muzzle. Choke constricts the bore and funnels shot into a concentrated mass as it exits the muzzle. Since choke occurs inside of the bore, it is not visible externally. When a shotgun is fired, that little cloud of lead pellets known as a shot column is contained in the bore as it travels down the barrel, and passes through the choke as it nears the muzzle. The constriction we call choke exerts radial forces on the pellets. Those forces push inward on the shot column, packing the pellets even more tightly as they prepare for entry into the big, wide world. Once the shot column exits the barrel, those radial forces are offset by natural forces such as air, wind, and gravity. These forces encounter the outer layer of pellets in the column first, battle the radial forces holding those pellets in a cluster,

SHOT PATTERN DIAGRAM

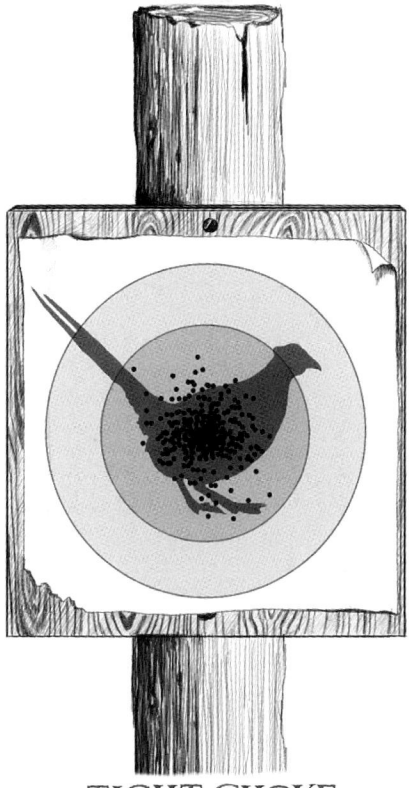

TIGHT CHOKE

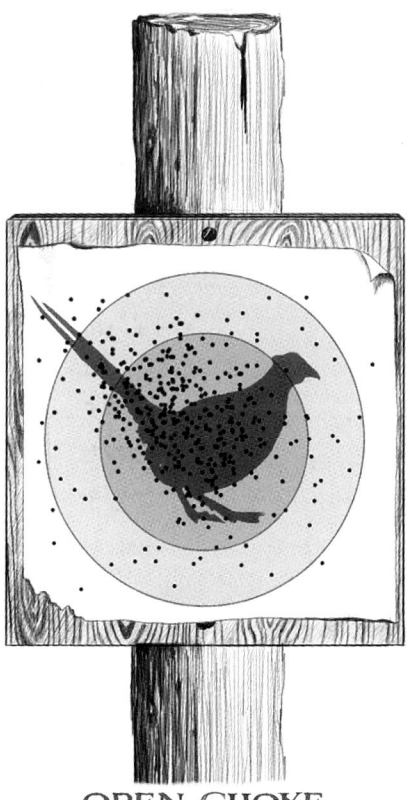

OPEN CHOKE

and cause them to zing off at tangents. This process initiates the widening of the pattern. Once the initial outer layer of pellets is shed, natural forces work on the newly established outer layer, and the process repeats itself with time and distance. In short, greater choke equals greater exertion of radial force, which is harder for the outside forces of nature to overcome, thereby maintaining the density of the shot column. This increase in radial force results in a tighter pattern. Hence, pellets forced through a tighter choke remain more tightly grouped for a longer period of time, and retain greater downrange killing potential for that reason.

But let's simplify:

lots of choke = pellets together = small pattern
little choke = pellets spread apart = big pattern

No constriction whatsoever, known as cylinder choke, provides the smallest exertion of radial force and allows for the most rapid dispersal of shot. In this constriction, or lack thereof, shot sprays from the barrel and spreads quickly into an ever-widening cloud. The greatest plausible constriction (i.e., full choke) exerts maximum radial force on the column and retains the shot in a tight cluster as it travels downrange.

Let's go back to the barn wall. This time, let's say we paint two Xs on the wall several feet apart. From forty yards, we fire a cylinder-choke barrel at the left-hand X, then, with an identical shell, we fire the full-choke barrel at the right-hand X. Upon examination, the left-hand X is peppered with a wider, more loosely concentrated pattern than the right-hand X. In shooting terms, the cylinder-choke barrel produced a more open pattern than the full-choke barrel, which produced a very tight pattern. But what does all of this barn shooting actually tell us (other than that the barn will need to be re-sided soon)?

From a hunter's standpoint, the tighter the choke, the more pellets that will coincide with

Damascus Barrels

As you delve deeper into guns, you will no doubt encounter heated discussions about Damascus barrels, and you will likely see a few in person. Damascus barrels are built by heating rods of steel and iron and twisting them into a pliable metal twist. This twist is then further heated and wrapped tightly around a mandrel or rod, which has been machined to the inside dimensions of the barrel. The resulting spiral is again heated and hammered together on the mandrel, effectively welding component parts into a single unit, from which the mandrel is removed. After final fitting and polishing, the surface takes on a beautiful tight pattern of interlaced metals. This intricate pattern is the signature of Damascus barrels.

Damascus barrels have gotten a bad rap in recent years for being dangerous. This premise stems from the fact that iron and steel, the components of the barrels, do not knit together to create a structure inherently capable of containing the high pressures associated with modern shotgun loads or shells. So too, iron and steel can degrade differently over time, presenting weak spots in the twist that are barely noticeable to the naked eye. The potential for accidents does indeed exist with Damascus barrels, and the fluid steel barrels of a modern gun may be the safer bet for a beginning shooter. That said, many Damascus-barreled guns are safely shot with light-pressure loads, simply because they have been proofed to do so. Proofing, accomplished in a secure testing facility known as a proof house, is the process of firing a load through the barrels that generates considerably higher pressures than any standard, or feasible, field load. In short, don't fear Damascus, but don't seek it out without sufficient education on the subject.

the bird, at greater range. A big, heavily feathered bird like a Dakota pheasant, which tends to run and flush ahead of a dog, might present a thirty-yard shot at something hard to penetrate (remember the heavily feathered part?). For a hunter to maximize the likelihood of killing this bird, said hunter might opt for a tighter choke than the one he or she would use when shooting a tiny, thin-skinned woodcock at a range of ten yards. On the other hand, if a hunter shot an open-choke barrel at a tough, fast-departing sharptail grouse from thirty-five Montana yards, said hunter might or might not seat a random pellet in that sharptail's rump. Said pellet might lack the killing power of multiple coincident pellets shot from a tighter-choke barrel. More pellets hitting in concert will do said sharptail the service of a humane kill, and provide the hunter with a lovely dinner; a single pellet may not. Generally, the bigger, more densely feathered birds, which are shot in open cover that makes for longer shots, require tighter chokes.

Traditional shotguns are fitted with an integral or fixed choke, which is machined into the

SHOTGUN CHOKE	YARDS	SHOTGUN CHOKE RESTRICTION (diameter difference between bore and shotgun choke in inches)
Cylinder	< 20	0
Skeet	22.5	.005
Improved Cylinder	25	.010
Light Modified	30	.015
Modified	32.5	.020
Improved Modified	35	.025
Light Full	37.5	.030
Full	40 or more	.035
Extra Full	40 or more	.040

bore. Modern guns, and some retrofitted classic guns, may have screw-in choke tubes that thread into the muzzle end of the bore, allowing shooters to change the degree of shot constriction dependent on the purpose. Choke designations refer to the amount of constriction of the bore diameter, presented for our purposes in inches. This constriction remains fairly constant among gauges. Standard choke designations are shown in the accompanying chart.

New guns, fitted with removable choke tubes, should come complete with the following choke tubes, listed in ascending order of constriction: cylinder, improved cylinder, modified, improved modified, and full.

Shotguns have historically been, and remain, available in double-barreled configurations, with barrels either aligned side-by-side or over/under. The beauty of two barrels lies in the fact that two chokes are available within one package, and the hunter who misses the first shot with the open choke retains good odds for a longer shot with his or her tighter-choke second shot. From a physics standpoint, this makes good sense; when a quail covey rises underfoot, a solid hit from a full-choke barrel, at something like ten yards, would result in little more than a haze of blood and feathers. What's more, the shot pattern at ten yards would be so tightly concentrated that it would be challenging for anything other than a squarely centered shot to hit the bird. The same shot taken with a cylinder choke would allow greater opportunity for a hit due to a larger initial pattern. Moreover, with less density to the pattern, far fewer pellets would impact the bird, thereby retaining some meat. But during said first shot, the remainder of the covey has continued to depart. Birds may now be twenty-five yards out, requiring an improved cylinder or modified choke to create the same pattern that a cylinder choke created at ten yards. See what I mean? Two barrels afford two chokes, and oftentimes, greater effect in the field.

Working back from the muzzle, the barrel is simply a metal tube. The wall or structure of the tube is called the barrel wall, and over much of

its length, the barrel wall is uniformly thick. Wall thickness is critical as it pertains to safety because a barrel wall has to be suitably thick to manage the pressure of a tiny explosion. Pressures dissipate along the length of a barrel, so wall thickness generally increases with proximity to the chamber, where the initial explosion takes place. But let's not get ahead of ourselves. Modern barrels are made of fluid steel, which is blued or blacked as a means of protecting the metal. Bluing is a chemical process that changes the outside surface of the barrel, making it slightly more impervious to rust than raw steel, and provides that lovely, blue-black color.

Moving closer to the breech end of the barrel—that is to say the end opposite the muzzle—we get to the chamber. The chamber is the place where the shotshell seats for firing. The chamber length and width depends on the intended ammunition, with gauge referring to the width (diameter). Standard lengths of chamber are two-and-a-half inches for many older British guns, two-and-three-quarters inches for the vast majority of guns, three inches for heavy waterfowl or turkey guns, and three-and-a-half inches for a serious turkey or goose gun, for the hunter who isn't afraid of a little punishment. Forward of the chamber is the forcing cone, which funnels the shot into the barrel, propelling it forward in a tight column.

To top off the discussion of barrels, it would be a pity to forget about the rib. The top rib is a flat bar of metal that sits on top of the barrel. On an over/under there is a top rib, and on a side-by-side there is simply a rib between the barrels. The rib on a single-barreled gun, if present, is on top of the barrel. Ribs come in all shapes, sizes, and finishes. Most modern over/under guns exhibit what is called a vent rib, wherein the rib itself is raised above the barrel by spaced posts or risers. This separation supposedly expedites the dissipation of heat from the barrels. The muzzle end of the shotgun rib is typically adorned with a bead, which ostensibly assists the shooter as he or she visualizes the target (though proper shooting technique dictates that all a shooter should see is his or her target).

Barrel Dangers

Before we conclude the conversation about barrels, I'd be remiss if I didn't take the opportunity to mention what can be a hugely dangerous consequence of poor awareness. As mentioned, a tremendous amount of pressure is generated within the barrel when a shotshell is discharged. If an obstruction of any kind occludes the barrel during discharge, the force of the discharge can and will be forced outward, thereby rupturing the barrel wall at the point of least resistance. Such an explosion can and will also destroy anything in its path, including hands and fingers. This catastrophe occurs most often under two distinct circumstances.

When hunting in snow, a hunter with cold or wet hands can easily drop a shotgun. When a gun is dropped, the muzzle can get inadvertently plunged into the snow and plugged. Though loose snow can occasionally blow out of a barrel, densely packed snow cannot. When a barrel plugged with snow is fired, the result is often a muzzle-end peeled back like a banana. This condition can be readily avoided if hunters check gun barrels regularly for blockages (from the breech end of course) or cover the muzzle with a small patch of rubberized electrical or duct tape. This patch will be useful in keeping snow out of the barrel, but will blow off easily in the event that the gun is discharged for a shot.

Of greater potential danger is a situation that has ruined a good number of guns—and upland hunters—over the years. Many shooters have in their quivers multiple gauges of gun. A twelve gauge for pheasants and ducks often lives in the same rack as a sweet little twenty for quail. The owner therefore likely has ammunition for both guns, and may keep a mixture of ammunition in the same vest pocket. This mixing of gauges can prove, and has proven, disastrous.

A twenty-gauge shell will slip easily into the barrel of a twelve-gauge gun. It will slide beyond the forcing cone and into the barrel. It will lodge there, far enough out of sight that the chamber will appear empty, as if the gun is not yet loaded. If the mistake is not recognized and rectified immediately, and a twelve-gauge shell is then loaded into the chamber and fired, a two-stage explosion ensues. Not only will the force of the twelve-gauge discharge not escape the barrel, but likely the force of the twelve-gauge shot will detonate the twenty-gauge cartridge deep in the barrel, causing compounding damage. This seemingly unlikely condition occurs far more regularly than any of us care to admit.

To sidestep this potentially deadly situation, keep twelve- and twenty-gauge ammo separate at all times. Moreover, when loading a barrel after a break, or after the gun has been stored, make a cursory check down the barrel to ensure that daylight shines through. When I pick up a shotgun, I always open the action and look down the barrels from the breech end. This has become second nature, and I hope this little exercise keeps me from ever falling prey to an obstructed barrel.

This image illustrates what can happen when a shell of inappropriate (smaller) gauge unknowingly slips down the barrel of a shotgun. The discharge of the next round creates incredible pressure, blowing out the steel walls of the barrel. Note that the shells visible in this image are dummy rounds, used to illustrate the danger.

ACTION

The barrel seats into a piece of metal known as the action or receiver. This component of the shotgun serves several purposes, mainly to house the spring-loaded hammer that acts upon the firing pin, and then upon the primer to induce discharge of the shotshell. A system of cocking holds the hammer under spring pressure, and the hammer is released by means of a trigger. The action may also incorporate a system to eject a spent (fired) shell, and insert a fresh shell into the chamber. There are three primary types of shotgun action used by upland hunters: break action, pump action, and semi-automatic action.

The mechanical workings of a shotgun can be complex from a design and engineering standpoint, and though the intricacies of shotgun "guts" are interesting, they can also be confusing. For our purposes, let's focus on the information needed to understand how to safely and effectively use a shotgun in the field.

Break-action shotguns fall into either the single-shot, side-by-side, or over/under category. This design incorporates a hinge pin upon which the barrels rotate (down) to expose the breech. Basically, in a break-action gun, a lever is depressed, which allows the barrels to tilt down, exposing the chambers for loading. Shells are placed manually within the chambers, the barrels are lifted back into place, a latch system holds the barrels in contact with the action, and the firing pins are able to act upon the primers.

Break-action guns are classic, time honored, and, by some measures, universally simple. Orvis has long championed break-action guns, both side-by-side and over/under models, for their elegance and utility. Their greatest attributes, however, lie in their innate safety features. Any and all shotguns engender some degree of hazard. The only surefire way to eliminate the potential of an accidental discharge is to "open" the action, thereby physically moving the firing pin away from the primer. The beauty of a break-action gun is that the hunter can slip a shell or two into the chambers, and walk quite comfortably with the action open. Hunters, guides, and bystanders can see by the articulated angle of the barrel in relation to the stock that the action is open and therefore inherently safe. Guides like this. Fellow hunters like this. The visible safety features of a break-action gun are a strong selling point for many first-time gun buyers, and rightly so. Break-action guns also have the distinction of being elegant, old-fashioned, and dripping with romance.

Pump-action or slide-action shotguns have a single barrel, underneath which is a secondary tube. This secondary tube is called a magazine, and it is where multiple shells are housed. The pump-action shotgun is loaded by filling the magazine through a port on the bottom of the receiver. The fore-end of the shotgun is a handle of sorts attached to the slide, and it is moved manually back toward the receiver

then forward toward the muzzle to seat a shell in the chamber. Affixed to the slide is the bolt, which is a cylindrical piece of steel in which the firing pin is housed. Once the shell is fired, the slide is manually cycled back, thereby pulling the spent shell out of the chamber, and ejecting it either out the side or the bottom of the receiver. As the spent shell is ejected, a fresh one is pushed from the magazine and engaged by the slide. When the slide cycles forward, it pushes this fresh shell into the chamber, cocks the hammer or firing pin, and the firing process is repeated.

Most pump-action shotguns hold five rounds between the chamber and the magazine. This multi-shot capacity is a selling point for certain, as is the comparatively low price point of many pump-action guns. The challenge with pump guns is the necessity of a significant mechanical action to cycle a round. After a shot is fired, the shooter must make the slide travel back and then forward, which at best takes time and at worst moves the gun barrel out of line with a departing bird. Though many claim that with time a slide-action gun can be cycled with blinding speed, effective handling does require practice and coordination.

From a safety standpoint, a slide-action gun is safe only when the slide is back toward the receiver, and the action is "open." In this case, an open action shows an ejection port on the side or base of the receiver that is both open (not filled by the metal of the bolt) and empty of a cartridge.

The semi-automatic action, also called an autoloader, is favored by many for its simplicity of use and its high-tech personality. A semi-auto is set up quite similarly to a pump, with a tubular magazine beneath the single barrel, a loading port on the base of the receiver, and an ejection port on the side. When a semi-auto is fired, however, the force of the

shot ejects the spent shell, forces the bolt back to grasp a new shell from the magazine, and loads that new shell into the chamber. In essence, the action is similar to that of the pump, but a combination of springs, compression, and inertia cycle the action automatically for the shooter. This cycle occurs at blinding speed, and multiple shots can be accomplished in seconds. An added value for the shooter is that much of the recoil gets absorbed in the process of cycling a round, resulting in less direct impact to be soaked up by the shooter's shoulder.

The problem with semi-autos is that, due to the complexity of the action, a lot can go wrong. Though there are exceptional and ingenious designs out there, anything with lots of moving parts opens the door for greater potential failure. Shells may not load or eject properly, or the shell that is entering the chamber may intercept the one exiting, resulting in a jam at a potentially inopportune time. Semi-automatic actions can also be a challenge to clean adequately, as they require disassembly for routine maintenance. Finally, as with a pump gun, an open action can be hard to see from a distance. I have more than once lifted a semi-auto from the rack and, upon opening the action (a necessary first when handling any firearm), ejected a live round. Shells seem to hide in semi-autos, and hidden shells are scary. But lest I poo-poo the semi-automatic action too much, it must be said that a good one cycles like silk and affords a quick third shot while the gun is still swinging.

■ STOCK

The stock of a shotgun is composed of two parts: the buttstock and the fore-end or forearm. The buttstock is the piece of the shotgun that marries to your shoulder and cheek, and allows the trigger hand a grip. The fore-end serves differing functions depending on action type, but in loose terms it provides a home for the forward hand that supports and guides the barrels. Shotgun stocks are historically constructed of walnut, which is both strong to absorb the abuse of recoil and light for ease of carrying. Modern guns can and often do have stocks made of various synthetics, which, to my eye, look out of place in the uplands.

The buttstock of the shotgun has several identifiable parts, namely the wrist, grip, comb, butt, heel, and toe, defined thus:

- **Wrist:** the region grasped by the trigger hand, very similar to the grip.

- **Grip:** somewhat synonymous with wrist, but used to designate the shape of the grip itself. The three primary shapes are pistol grip, prince-of-wales/round knob grip, or straight grip.

- **Comb:** the top line of the buttstock; contacts the cheek of the shooter.

- **Butt:** the face of the rear of the buttstock; contacts the shoulder of the shooter. Often covered in a plastic buttplate or rubber/leather recoil pad.

- **Heel and toe:** top and bottom of the butt, respectively.

After some period, the new shotgunner will encounter a discussion of gun fit. Gun fit describes the dimensions of the buttstock, and the implication that, as in clothing, not all guns fit all shooters. Gun fit is another conversation entirely, but the measurements of a stock are worth understanding. The pertinent stock measurements are length of pull, drop, and cast. They are defined thus:

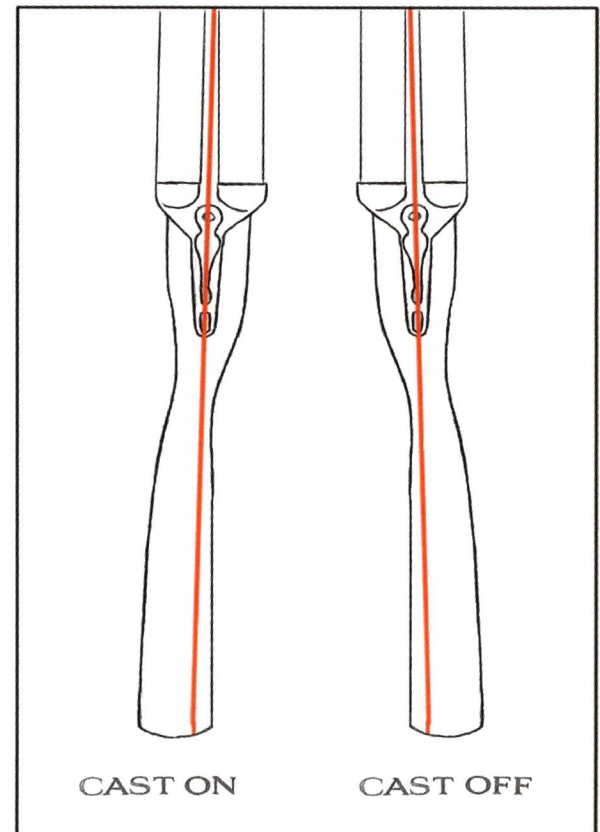

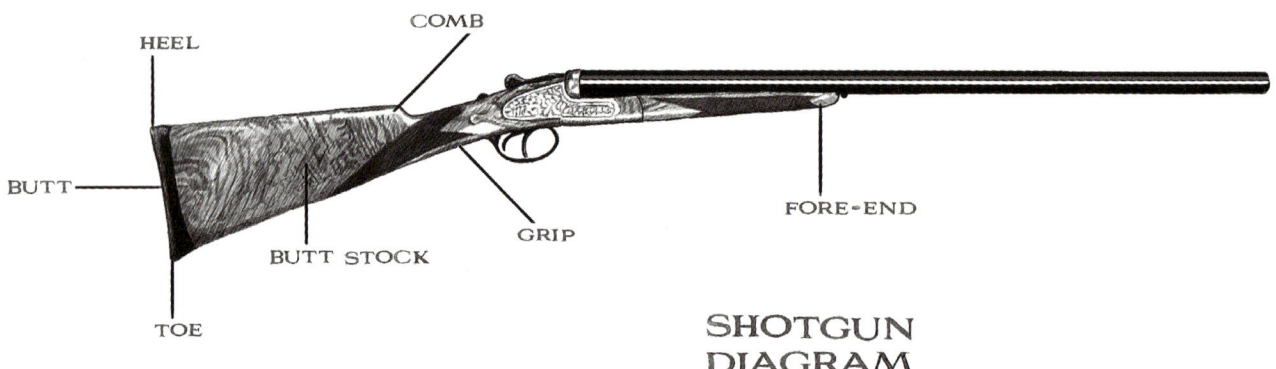

SHOTGUN DIAGRAM

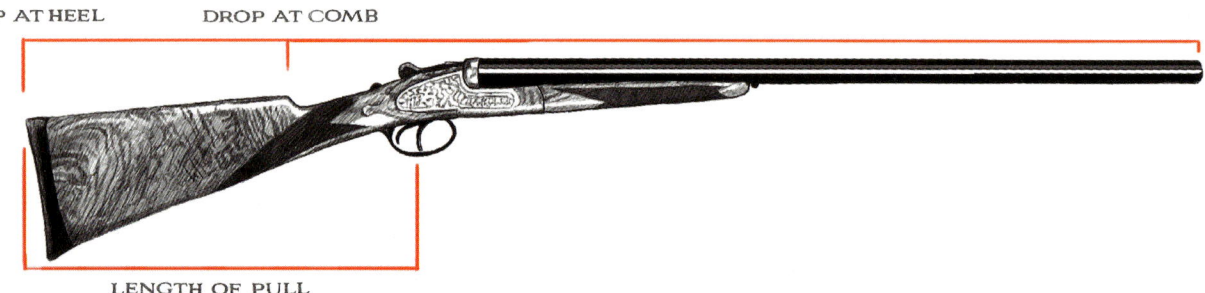

Lock, Stock, and Barrel

Shotguns are magnificent and exciting tools, and I've described them here in perhaps greater depth than necessary. That said, a working understanding of the technicana of guns can serve to make them slightly less intimidating for a new hunter. What's more, fellow shooters, guides, and would-be hunting partners are often affirmed when the person walking beside them with a gun in hand has a solid understanding of how that gun works and the potential damage it gun can do. Armed with information, a new gun handler can be a safe gun handler, and avail himself more readily to the wonderful task at hand.

- **Length of pull:** the distance from the front trigger to the center of the butt.

- **Drop at comb:** extent of vertical offset between the top of the barrels (rib) and the comb of the buttstock.

- **Drop at heel:** extent of vertical offset between the top of the barrels (rib) and the heel of the buttstock.

- **Cast:** extent of offset left (cast on) or right (cast off) between the midline of the barrels and the center of the butt.

The fore-end is a far easier bit of the stock to describe. It is simply a piece of wood affixed to the barrels or action, providing a place for the forward hand to grasp. In side-by-side shotguns, a slim, insubstantial fore-end is known as a splinter fore-end, and a chunkier, wider-than-the-barrels fore-end is called a beavertail fore-end.

Decisions, Decisions

You are now equipped with a sound understanding of shotguns and their practicality as it pertains to upland hunting. That said, you are likely no more clear about which shotgun would most make sense for you with regard to your intended hunting. I'll be the first to tell you that over the years, I have grown into something of a shotgun snob, with a distinct predilection for the esoteric but nowhere near the funds to back up my tastes. I therefore have bought and sold and traded my fair share of guns that were slightly "off" in more ways than one. Had I only been willing to buy a sound and practical gun early on, I likely would have saved a heap of money and shot more birds to boot. But I'm no pragmatist, and you may not be either. If used guns, classic guns, old guns, or odd guns pique your interest, brace yourself for a wild ride. If you'd like something serviceable, practical, and deadly, then follow my advice here; I have more than enough mistakes under my belt to inform the opinions I'll share.

If you are buying a first gun, don't be afraid to spend some money. A tool designed to become a working part of you, a trusted companion, and something capable of honorably taking a life is a tool of value, present and future. Buy something sound and safe, something dynamic and beautiful to your eye, and something that fits both your physique and the aesthetic you've begun to create for yourself. In general, all of these needs can be met with a new, or lightly used, twenty-gauge over/under, fitted with three-inch chambers, twenty-eight-inch barrels, and screw-in chokes. Such a gun can be had from a handful of makers, but trust the big names; they've become so for good reason. A serviceable, used over/under can be had for somewhere between $1,000 and $2,000 at the time of this writing. That said, for a few hundred dollars more, Orvis's proprietary ELOS shotgun is a strikingly sweet gun.

The practicality of the described gun is undeniable. A twenty gauge, especially with three-inch chambers, will adeptly harvest anything from close-range woodcock to a ptarmigan in a tailwind, depending on what shells you feed it. Twenty-eight-inch barrels swing fluidly on the clays course or in the pheasant fields, but are not so long as to be cumbersome in tight cover. Interchangeable chokes can follow you from the quail fields to the grouse woods to the (dare I say it?) duck blind, allowing for clean kills across the venues. An off-the-rack new modern gun fits most men, and can be easily modified to fit most women or youngsters by a routine shortening of the stock. A twenty-gauge field gun, weighing in at around six pounds, is trim, light, and easy to carry all day. Most importantly, an over/under enables new hunters, and their companions, the confidence of seeing an open action, empty chambers, and an inherently safe gun. This feature alone, to my mind, is worth a week's wages on the price tag.

If you, like me, cannot be swayed by practicality, things get more complicated. If you are a rigid traditionalist, you'll want a side-by-side. This desire will make your spouse look at you aghast when you first enter the gun shop together and review the prices. Side-by-side shotguns from the better makers are worth their weight in gold, and we've begun to see an overvaluation of even the working-grade guns. If you must have one, follow the advice of a knowledgeable and trustworthy gun salesman and then buy used. American guns by Ithaca, Winchester, Stevens, and Savage, as well as lower-grade Italian or Spanish guns, can be had for less than the price of a new over/under. You'll wind up with a twelve gauge most likely, so be prepared for a heavy, long-barreled gun.

Given my druthers, I'd rather see new hunters with a fitted gun. The process of developing shooting skills, and the plausible result of birds in the bag, will be hastened by a gun that fits the shooter. A fitted gun, like a fitted suit, marries perfectly to the body of its owner. A fitted gun, also like a fitted suit, hinges upon a fitting, which computes stock dimensions that allow the gun to naturally point where the shooter is looking. A proper fitting is best accomplished by a trained gunfitter, though this process can be both expensive and time consuming.

Orvis and several other shooting schools offer gunfitting as a component of the educational process. A fitting employs the use of a try gun, which has a stock equipped with numerous adjustments that enable limitless customization. As the try gun is adjusted, the shooter fires repeatedly at a patterning board, which is simply a clean, whitewashed sheet of metal. Adjustments are made to ensure that the point of impact coincides with the shooter's visual target, and the resulting dimensions are recorded. Once dimensions are obtained, a gun can be custom built, or custom retrofitted, to meet the exact needs of the shooter. Generally, this customization is accomplished on a higher-end gun, with the fitting rolled in to the end cost. As of this writing, $3,500 to $5,000 will put a shooter into a lovely, fitted gun that will point like a laser beam and encourage solid shooting fundamentals. A fit gun is a pleasure and a comfort to shoot, and should by all means be considered if the resources allow.

If a pump or a semi-auto is bestowed upon you, don't necessarily turn up your nose. Certainly, these guns are serviceable, and may become lifelong companions. Simply be aware that pumps and semi-autos are only truly safe when the action is open, and that open action can be hard to ascertain, especially from a distance. Moreover, some preserves or lodges will not allow hunters in the field with any gun that does not have a break action, or any gun larger than twenty gauge.

Practicality and Necessity: The Legal Aspects

So you've decided to become a hunter, you've taken a shooting lesson, you have even set your sights on the purchase of a lovely new over/under twenty gauge. Fall is fast approaching, and you hear that there are pheasants on some public land in the western part of the state. Looks like it's time to buy that gun, get a few shells, and go out hunting!

Or . . . maybe not. Game laws and gun laws dictate what sort of licensure is required before you purchase a gun or shoot a bird. Generalizations about rules and regulations are hard to make, as laws vary significantly from state to state. In the paragraphs that follow, I'll make what recommendations I can to ensure that you operate within the boundaries of the law.

Gun Laws

State and federal laws dictate the safe and legal purchase, possession, and transport of firearms and ammunition. State police agencies, or even state websites, are often the best resource for local regulations. In general, when you attempt to buy a firearm from a licensed dealer, you will be informed about any laws that impact the purchase and sale. In some states, buying a first shotgun is about as easy as buying a pack of cigarettes, but it is best to be informed about legal transport and legal discharge (shooting). Again, local and state police agencies are responsible for enforcing these laws, and therefore should be a sound source of guidance.

If a gun is given to you, or if you hope to borrow a gun, definitely look into the local regulations. Gun laws are taken quite seriously in most states, and a pledge of ignorance does little when there's an undocumented twelve gauge and a box of shells in the backseat.

Game and Hunting Laws

As I mentioned, I took my hunter's safety course in rural Vermont, in the dining hall of the local middle school. A French-Canadian dairy farmer taught the course, and took it upon himself to bombard me with unanswerable questions throughout, much to the amusement of the rest of the student body, whose average age was eleven. In that part of the world, kids started hunting early, and my late arrival to hunting prompted a lot of giggles from my class-

mates and their rough-handed fathers. Though the experience of sitting through the class was humbling, it was a necessary evil: state law required proof of hunter's education before I was ever to hunt birds legally, and the fall was fast approaching. So I did my time, and smoked out a near-perfect score on the final exam (the one I got wrong was a trick question, I swear!). Upon passing the exam I was free, and I've carried the little orange card that verifies my legality proudly ever since.

Most states require completion of a state-certified hunter's safety course prior to the purchase of a hunting license. Different states have different mandates along these lines, but generally speaking, a certain number of classroom hours, followed by a written exam, establish a degree of proficiency and safety for the would-be hunter. Some states allow for the option of studying independently outside of the classroom, and then sitting for the test. This option is often a better bet for the adult hunter, as the majority of hunter's safety courses—in more rural areas especially—are geared to a very young student body.

Hunter's safety courses can be a challenge to find, depending on your region. State fish and game departmental websites generally serve as a good resource for finding a public offering, and many states also provide a list of instructors willing to teach a course on demand, though often for a fee. Once the course is completed, however, and a verification card awarded, you are in the clear for life. If by chance the hunter's safety card is lost, a previous year's license or a license from another state is often proof enough of completion. That said, it is best to laminate the card and keep it in your wallet, lest any question arise concerning your eligibility for licensure. In addition, you should record the number associated with your hunter's safety certification in a place where it won't be easily lost. With this number and the state of completion, a card can generally be reissued.

Once a hunting license is legally purchased, be certain that all applicable add-ons are purchased as well. In many states, a small-game hunting license is all that is needed to hunt upland birds. That said, the addition of a "conservation stamp" or other

fee might be necessary, as might specific stamps for certain bird species. American woodcock are a migratory game bird, and therefore occupy a bit of a gray area where licensure is concerned. If hunting woodcock, be sure to obtain a Harvest Information Program (HIP) number, so that successful records of woodcock harvests can be kept.

The Preserve Option

I will go into greater depth about hunting preserves in a later chapter, but in short, preserves might be the greatest introductory opportunity for the newly minted upland hunter. Licensed preserves, occupying privately held land, generally require hunters to possess no state or federal licensure. Hunters can literally arrive and start shooting, whether or not they've ever held a hunting license or taken a hunter's safety course. Preserves also often offer gun rentals, making the challenges of shotgun possession moot. On occasion, preserve hunters are required to purchase a preserve license, additional to the cost of the hunt itself.

Preserves have gotten a bad rap historically as being fly-by-night, backyard operations with limited cover and poor-flying birds. Indeed, this can still be the case, but increasingly I am seeing some of the finest upland opportunities in North America taking place on preserves. For the aspiring hunter, or the individual who wants to "try it out" before committing to a gun purchase and a hunter's safety course, a preserve offers a perfect venue. Moreover, the preserve season in most states extends well beyond the state-mandated hunting seasons and allows a wider range of dates for would-be hunters.

For fear of indicating that preserves are overrun with neophyte hunters, let me clarify that almost any preserve of repute requires that hunters follow a clearly established set of safety guidelines. Just because licensure is not required does not mean that an overarching focus on safety is chucked out the window. To the contrary, many preserves require the viewing of an in-depth safety video that provides guidelines specific to safe hunting on the preserve property.

Dressing the Part

 Chapter 5

Dressing the Part

In my thinking about hunting gear, I return continually to the words of the late Norman Maclean who, though most readily identified as a fly fisherman, grew up in a rich hunting tradition. In *A River Runs Through It*, Maclean reflects that "although I have never pretended to be a great fisherman, it was always important to me that I *was* a fisherman and *looked* like one." I relate to Maclean on so many levels, most notably in the assertion that appearance and identity can become closely entwined and not always in a negative manner. I too love to look like what I identify as being, particularly in the uplands during bird-hunting time.

I have a friend in southern Vermont for whom the pomp and circumstance of upland hunting is, quite possibly, the whole point. He owns a closet full of pressed brush pants for the quail fields, bespoke tweeds for European pheasant drives, and safari-style poplin shirts and short pants for his forays to the African savannah. Dressing the part, for this man anyway, is both an art form and a science.

Do not overlook for a moment the value or validity of gearing up. It is an enjoyable process in itself, and it can and will impact the success, safety, and comfort of your days afield. That said, when coming into this process cold, the array of gear options that stretch from guns to gum boots can seem more than a bit overwhelming. Depending on the region, or the type of cover to be hunted, clothing choices can vary. I'll attempt, in the following paragraphs, to shed some light on the best choices for the upland hunter and the variances that might be considered. I'll also do my best to suggest clothing and gear options that will enable your guide and gunning buddies to confidently occupy the barstool beside you without worrying that their credibility might be compromised.

Boots

A guide in Texas once told me that he can size up his client in one glance by looking at his or her boots. He claims that a hunter who arrives in a brand-new, fresh-from-the-box pair of boots never fails to make him nervous. My friend went on to assert that on the mild end of the spectrum, new boots foretell blisters by the day's end, while on the other extreme, they point toward a hunter who may be dangerously inexperienced. In any case, he's leery of "new boot" hunters and goes to great lengths to get low when such hunters start shooting.

Perhaps prejudices based on boot choice are, like most prejudices, somewhat unfair, but they no doubt exist. For this reason, choose your boots wisely and wear them prior to the advent of the hunting day. In the end, upland hunting is an activity that revolves around a shootable gun and a pair of good boots. The rest, to a large degree, is just pageantry.

In New England, the weather can be variable and the terrain unforgiving. Generally, grouse and

woodcock hunters set out prepared for slick leaves, mud, fallen trees, alder bottoms, and significant hills. For this reason, rubber boots with a sturdy lug sole, or a shin-high boot of well-oiled leather, are the best options. I have also, in recent years, taken to wearing sturdy, waterproof hiking boots for my fair-weather grouse hunting, as they keep me dry and provide the traction I need for clearing blowdowns and streambeds. Though I've liked the support and nimble feel of the hikers, I've probably spent more hunting days in rubber boots than anything else.

I can't help but take this opportunity to elucidate that all rubber boots are *not* made equally. For much of my life, I lived in agricultural communities, and I would often trundle out of the woodcock coverts and into the barn just in time for an afternoon of milking. I went through every conceivable make and model of rubber boot, and I wore them the whole year through. By virtue of this testing process, I determined that though they are not inexpensive, a natural latex, Wellington-type boot is hands-down the finest rubber boot available. Companies such as Aigle, Le Chameau, and Hunter make a boot such as this, and you will no doubt be struck by the price tag. But natural latex has a way of stretching and moving, resealing small punctures, and remaining impervious to cracking. A good pair of natural rubber boots will survive several years of hard wear, and, under moderate use, will last a lifetime.

Cold-weather hunters in the North and Midwest have had good recent success with lug-soled boots with neoprene uppers made by companies such as Muck Boot and Bogs. These styles work well for many. They are warm, waterproof, and high enough to offer ample protection. They are also relatively light for their bulk, and can be rolled down in warmer weather.

Hunters who pursue mountain or desert birds in rugged, craggy terrain might benefit from a true mountain boot. Such a boot has a lug sole,

a protected toe, a steel shank, and ample ankle support. Breathability can be a necessity in such a boot, and Gore-Tex or other waterproof breathable construction is warranted. Think of something like a beefed-up hiking boot, and don't be afraid of blending leather and synthetics to reduce weight. Kenetrek and Meindl lead the league in this discipline, and you'll go wrong with neither.

Where the cover is flat and minimally log strewn, a lighter-weight boot with a less aggressive tread can be a blessing. Traditional, moc-toe models by Gokey, Orvis, Russell Moccasin, Weinbrenner, and Irish Setter are light and comfortable, and possess a certain handmade elegance. They are comfortable when broken in properly, and, with a good application of Sno-Seal, can be fairly waterproof. They are, in many ways, the ideal prairie or plantation boot, and they certainly fit with that aesthetic. When hunting in certain southern regions, however, the addition of a snakeproof gaiter, or a tall snakeproof boot upper, can be a worthwhile precaution.

DRESSING THE PART ■ 91

And then of course there are socks. Socks are undervalued by most hunters, but taken quite seriously by guides and professionals. A good pair of socks maintains its integrity, fails to slip and bunch, and wicks moisture. Regardless of temperature, I'm a wool man through and through, and I'm a huge fan of the technical merino offerings from companies like Darn Tough, Orvis, and Smartwool. Whatever your sock choice, make certain they are tall enough to reach well above the boot top and snug enough to stay in place. Break in boots with appropriate socks, and don't be afraid to wear a silk liner sock to prevent blisters.

Pants

Brush pants are central to the upland gunner's kit. A traditional pair is cut like jeans or chinos, but boasts a reinforced front to protect the hunter from briars, brush, and impediments such as barbed wire. Good brush pants wear like armor, and when needed, they can be a lifesaver. That said, they can also wear quite literally like armor, proving heavy, stiff, and cumbersome. When it comes to pants, the upland hunter should consider his or her environment and plan accordingly.

A solid option, where convention allows, is simply a pair of jeans or work pants. Where the cover is thin and short, and the prevalence of thorns minimal, true brush pants—though "cool" in the colloquial sense—are unnecessary. The vast majority of wild bird guides in the Mountain West settle for double-front Carhartt work pants or Wrangler jeans, and they wear them religiously through the bird season. That said, they are not often plagued by morning dew, snags, or heavy frosts. They know their environment and dress to meet it.

In midwestern pheasant country, hunters encounter standing grain, ditch grasses, and corn. Morning frost and dew can be substantial, as can drifting snow. In pheasant country, a serious pair of waterproof breathable brush pants is a must, and it

will make any hunting day more enjoyable. In southeastern quail country, a pair of light, double-front brush pants is absolutely de rigueur and a critical piece of the regional costume, both for protection from native briars and as a nod to tradition. In the grouse woods, pants get torn to ribbons by thorn apple, rosebush, blackberry, and buckthorn; in such environs, brush pants are armor, quite literally.

In general, you can't go wrong with a pair of well-fitting, double-front brush pants. Orvis's tried and true Missouri Breaks pants have undergone periodic updates without ever being "improved" beyond recognition, and they are a perennial favorite. Consider the temperature and the potential for dew or frost in your hunting environment, and choose the style, material, and weight of your brush pants accordingly. Companies such as Orvis go to great lengths to provide a range of offerings that are regionally specific. In short, however, choose pants that will be warm, dry, and comfortable over the course of a long walking day; a considered pair of pants can be a godsend, and can look pretty darn snazzy as well.

Chaps

In an effort to confuse matters just a bit, let's discuss the viability of chaps. Chaps are basically waxed-cotton, canvas, or synthetic leggings that fit over a pair of pants and protect the legs like a pair of brush pants. The beauty of chaps is that they can be worn over any comfortable pair of pants, and can be removed and stored when not needed. A lightweight pair can be stashed in a vest pocket and carried discreetly, making little impact on the hunt or hunter.

Chaps are generally threaded through the belt that holds up the pants, and many are a one-size-fits-all proposition. Some have zippers at the cuff to allow for removal over boots, while others are simply straight legged with a finished cuff. Lightweight

DRESSING THE PART ■ 95

chaps of waterproof material can be worn during the wet of the morning and then removed when the sun dries the cover. Chaps are a worthwhile addition to any upland hunter's ensemble.

Shirts

Like pants, shirts should be chosen to suit the environment in which you hunt. A heavy, briar-resistant shooting shirt can save your arms in the grouse woods, whereas a short-sleeved poplin shirt can be a blessing in the South Texas scrub. Hard walking for mountain birds can necessitate an athletic, synthetic, wicking layer. Cover type, season, climate, and moisture potential all dictate the shirt choices of upland hunters.

My personal favorite New England hunting shirts are long-sleeved, button-down shirts made of boiled or worsted wool. They are thick and heavy enough to bust the briars, and they literally last two lifetimes. They can barely be ripped, they remain warm when wet, and they don't shrivel and melt around the post-hunt fire. Best of all, they don't require much washing.

Here is an opportunity, however, to open the conversation about hunter orange. Hunter, blaze, or safety orange is a high-visibility shade that stands out dramatically in most settings. It is employed widely in upland and big-game hunting clothing, because in both arenas maximum visibility is a critical component of safety. Camouflage, except in very specific situations, is not a concern for the upland hunter, as birds on the ground will flush due to proximity and physical disturbance rather than visual alerts. That said, particularly in thick cover, upland hunters should be hypervigilant about making their presence known to guides and hunting partners. Any lengths that a hunter can take to be visible add to the safety of the hunt and limit the potential for injury. Hunter orange, liberally worn, can assist

in this process. Moreover, many states require that upland hunters wear a minimum number of square inches of hunter orange specifically, as delineated in hunting abstracts. A safe bet is to always assume that hunter orange should be worn on the head and upper body; even where it is not mandated, it cannot hurt to maximize your visual presence.

Hunting shirts that are entirely orange, or at least applied with orange swatches, are widely available. Hunting brands such as Orvis ensure that the chosen shade is both appropriate for maximum effect and within the tonal ranges to be legally approved for hunting. Red, chartreuse, or other bright colors, though highly visible, may not be approved under state hunting laws. I have personally, on one occasion, been reprimanded by a game warden for wearing an orange hat that had faded into a dull shade unacceptable under Massachusetts hunting law.

Vests

My hunting mentor David W. Brown has a ragged, bloodstained, waxed-cotton vest that hangs on his woodshop wall. It is marked with a lifetime of memories and miles, and it's a powerful talisman for him and for me. I'd venture to say that he has worn the vest for the vast majority of his hunting days, and I don't think he'll ever own another. Dave, like many sportsmen of his generation, is just like that; he finds what he likes and sticks with it.

I, on the other hand, am more mercurial. I've had a small handful of hunting vests over the years, and I've yet to come close to wearing one out. I've bounced around in my selection for two reasons. First, I like gear. I like to buy new things, and try new things, and make my decisions from there. Second, as I've refined my hunting style and become more comfortable in the type of hunting I do, I've realized that my needs are more minimal than I once thought. Truth be told, it's a rare day in my New England when I'm required to carry more than two birds, a fistful of shells, and a compass.

Whatever your choice in vests, determine realistic use before buying. If you plan only to hunt bobwhites on a preserve in the company of a guide or dog handler, your needs are quite few. A light vest or pouch belt, applied with hunter orange, will more than suffice to carry shells, water, and the occasional small bird. Most bulky gear will be carried by the guide, and you will likely hunt fairly close to the truck or preserve buildings. If busting the brush in the grouse woods, something rugged and snag-free, as well as streamlined, will be a good choice. Think waxed cotton, pockets with secure closures, and a prevalence of orange. A strap vest, which lacks a full front and shoulders, can provide a lighter, more dynamic fit, but it won't necessarily provide much upper-body protection.

A vest should have, at the minimum, a large, rear, bloodproof game pouch and two front pockets for shells and other necessities. A zippered internal pocket for your license and wallet is a design feature that I appreciate. So too do I appreciate secure closures on the shell pockets that can be easily opened with one hand when reloading. I'm embarrassed to admit that I've unknowingly left a trail of shells across the uplands of this country due to shell pockets that never closed successfully. But I've also found myself in the second wave of a covey rise, fumbling with snaps as I tried in vain to reload. Some happy medium in this realm is necessary.

Most companies offer a guide model vest. This offering generally features larger carrying capacity for birds and water, accessories and compartments for electronics, and specific pockets for things such as first-aid equipment. Guide vests often are constructed with an internal suspension system to distribute the load and enable comfort of movement. I love to consider myself a pro, and I have to admit that in the past I've been sold on the concept of a guide model vest strictly for aspirational reasons. But I realized quickly that in running a single dog in tight cover for only a handful of shots, I was far overdressed in something designed for large and heavy loads. I trimmed things down to a slim, mesh strap vest, carried far fewer shells, and found that I was happier and more nimble moving through the hunting day.

Be cautious of the fittings on any vest that you buy. Vests designed with the shooter in mind have metal fittings that are covered with cloth or plastic. Exposed metal in certain areas on a vest can wreak havoc on a fine gun stock. Make certain that snaps or buttons are covered by pocket flaps, and that buckles are placed out of high-contact areas such as the shooting shoulder or chest.

DRESSING THE PART

Jackets

For some reason, I always seem to avoid wearing a jacket if at all possible. I like the minimalist ethos and the freedom of motion that comes from just a shirt paired with a light strap vest. When the cold or rain or snow threatens to keep me inside, however, I do what I must. I layer up and get after it, often glad for the warmth and protection of a heavy jacket.

Bulk can make shooting difficult, so upland hunting jackets should be chosen wisely. Heavy parkas are necessary when the Dakota winds howl in December pheasant fields, and waterproof jackets make the foul-weather grouse hunter a whole lot happier. In general, however, limit your layers where you can, and only wear as much of a jacket as you must. If you are warm gearing up by the truck, you'll be downright hot when you start walking. Shed a layer, start cool, and get your blood pumping to stay warm.

A windproof softshell jacket, such as Orvis's Upland Shell, is a wonderful all-around choice for the late season. It can be worn under a strap vest and remains breathable and dynamic over a range of conditions. Traditional waxed-cotton coats or jackets are tremendously hip and nearly bulletproof, but I absolutely cannot hunt in them. The lack of breathability and the rigidity of the fabric when cold make for an unpleasant experience. The durability of the fabric is great for dense and prickly cover, and no doubt generations of wet-weather hunters have sworn by waxed cotton; I simply can't make it work.

In tremendously wet conditions, a light waterproof or Gore-Tex jacket worn over an insulating layer might be the best bet. In general, though, expect to get a bit wet when hunting in heavy rain or wet woods. A full PVC rain suit, like those worn by commercial fishermen, lacks breathability and will soak you from within, as sweat gets trapped and cannot escape. Gore-Tex, though a magical fabric, eventually gets permeated with moisture. If hunting in extreme rain, remember that nature is a fickle friend. If you want to be out, expect to get wet, and insulate for warmth with synthetic layers; you are better off staying warm when wet than dealing with the poor insulative qualities of cotton. Cotton kills, as they say, and it is a bad choice for the foul-weather hunter.

In extreme cold, use a heavy hunting jacket in lieu of a vest altogether. Most upland product companies make a cold-weather jacket replete with a game pouch, shell pockets, and plenty of orange. Prairie and plains bird hunters who brave the late season often encounter bitter winds and occasion-

ally snow. Gear up against these conditions with thoughtful layering under a heavy, upland-specific coat, and you'll remain comfortable, or somewhat so. And if the weather is that bad, you should probably be duck hunting!

Accessories

Upland hunting, unlike so many other outdoor activities, is refreshingly lean on gimmicks and gadgets. As I said at the start of this chapter, a good pair of boots and a gun that fits are really all the upland hunter needs to succeed. There are a few niceties, however, that make for a more enjoyable, and indeed safer, day afield.

■ HATS

Hats for the upland hunter revolve around hunter orange. Many states require that a modicum of hunter orange be worn on the head, and blaze baseball caps have become standard issue. That said, there are other options: wide-brimmed felt hats, woolen or synthetic watch caps, even worsted Stormy Kromer–style brimmed caps—all made in hunter orange—are equally suitable choices. Different hat styles are selected based largely on weather and conditions, while also allowing the hunter a chance to express his or her personal style.

The consistent design element in upland hats is a brim of some sort to shade the eyes and protect the face from the sun. Only in extreme cold

do I swap a brimmed hat for a woolen watch cap, and even then I do so only under duress. Whatever your choice, consider adding to the headgear assembly a kerchief, neck gaiter, or buff in hunter orange, which can protect the neck from sun, dripping rain, or chill. Also make certain that square-inch requirements for orange upland headwear are met or exceeded for the state in which you hunt.

■ GLASSES

Glasses are a safety requirement for shooters at most preserves, lodges, or private hunting grounds, as well as at most clays facilities. They should be a universal safety requirement. Mandated or not, shooting glasses are never a bad idea, for a multitude of reasons. Foremost, shooting glasses protect your eyes from thorns, tree branches, blowing dust and particles, and on rare occasion stray pellets. For this reason, shooting glasses should offer good coverage, and should feature lenses made *not*

of glass, but of synthetic, impact-resistant material. Polycarbonate, or plastic-like material, retains sufficient integrity upon impact to withstand substantial force, while glass, though optically superior, can shatter. I'd not welcome pellets to the face under any circumstance, but the addition of glass shrapnel to such a blow would greatly exacerbate any potential injury. Wear glasses, and be certain they are designed for field use.

Shooting glasses should be selected based on fit, style, coverage, lens tint, and impact resistance. Measures of impact resistance for lenses have resulted in a graduation of levels, with mil-spec being the minimum recommended standard for a shooting lens.

Beyond safety considerations, shooting glasses, available in a variety of tints, can make for better contrast or sun suppression in the field. On sunny days, birds have a way of flying across the sun, and a smooth swing can be easily interrupted by an annoying few moments of blindness. On low-light days, when birds are flushing in the woods or against a mottled backdrop, a rose or vermillion lens tint can sharpen the sight picture. Granted, these features of lens tint are subjective to

104 ■ THE ORVIS GUIDE TO UPLAND HUNTING

the shooter, but if nothing else, clear lenses of mil-spec or better impact resistance really are a must for upland hunters.

■ HEARING PROTECTION

Hearing protection is not a necessity, but it's very much recommended. In all honesty, the three best shots I know all wear hearing aids, due in large part to decades afield and on the range without adequate hearing protection. I can say that though I cherish my hearing, and in effect would rather deplete a host of other senses if my hearing were to remain intact, I am pretty bad about wearing ear protection. My reasoning on this front is that my spatial awareness is thrown off when I can't hear a flush or a wing-beat, and in turn my shooting suffers. Fortunately, modern technology provides a solution even for this problem.

Several companies now make both in-ear and muff-type sound-suppression devices that operate in such a way that sharp noises such as gunshots are suppressed while human voices, conversational speech, and wing-beats are not. Though such devices are not cheap, and in-ear plugs, particularly custom-fit models, can range upward of $1,000 per pair, that sum seems a small price to pay for a lifetime of hearing. But there are, of course, other options.

Simple, expandable foam earplugs, or their more robust rubber counterparts, are more than sufficient for field and range use. Almost all guides carry a pair for their clients, and most shooting or pro shops have a bin full of them. These plugs are widely available at hardware or drug stores as well, and can be bought in bulk. I always have a pair or two on hand in my vest or glasses case, and I've grown much better about actually wearing them in the field. I've found that under most conditions visual cues provide sufficient indication of flushes, enabling shooters to pick up and swing without relying too heavily on hearing. If you are hunting over dogs, a staunch pointer or birdy flusher will also be a stellar indicator of birds, rendering hearing somewhat moot. Bottom line? Wear plugs, muffs, or some sort of hearing protection; you'll be pleased in the long run that you did.

■ GLOVES

Gloves are an accessory much overlooked by many upland gunners. Indeed, in fine weather and open cover nothing provides as much "feel" to the shooter as a bare hand. That said, in cold weather or thorny cover, or situations in which ample shooting can result in hot gun barrels, a shooting glove of some sort is a necessary accessory. A good pair of shooting gloves should provide "feel" and sensitivity while remaining rugged enough to provide some protection. A sufficient cuff is a feature that should not be overlooked, as wrists take a beating in dense cover.

In cold-weather conditions, it is tempting to opt for a thick, heavy glove. I often fear that, in doing so, a gunner will compromise enough sensitivity to make safe gun handling cumbersome. That said, cold hands are senseless and also make for inefficient handling, and therein lies the challenge. I wear thin leather gloves whenever possible, at least until significant cold sets in. I buy them to fit snug, and I often waterproof them with Sno-Seal or mink oil. Orvis makes a beautiful pair of deerskin shooting gloves that is thin yet remarkably strong; goatskin I find too soft to be of much use over the long haul. Golf gloves or batting gloves can prove

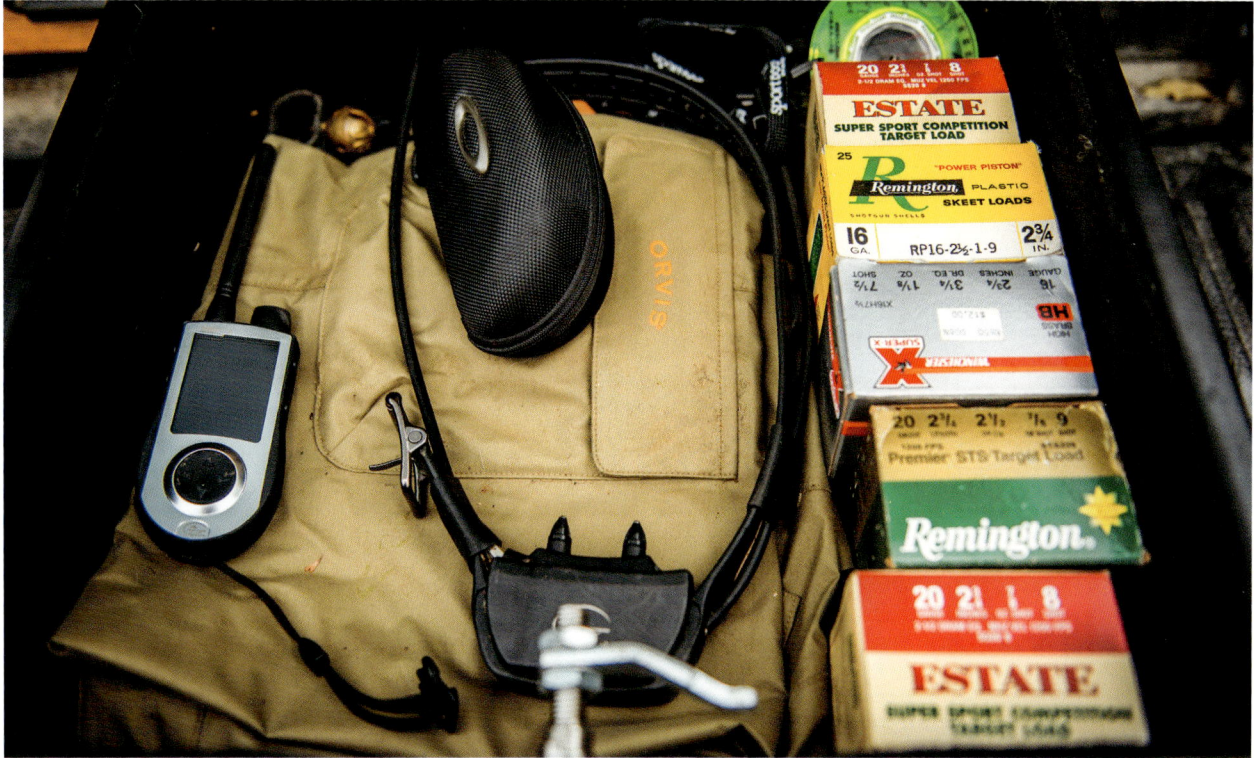

similarly effective, though they somehow lack the aesthetic appropriateness of a true shooting glove. When winter looms, I move to a slightly thicker, lined deerskin glove or a technical shooting glove of synthetic material. The latter, though somewhat modern for my taste, retains sensitivity while adding warmth, and as a perpetually cold person, I appreciate any warmth I can get! In the coldest weather, though I'm tempted to wear a heavy glove, I resist when I can. I'd rather feel my gun effectively than fumble around when firearms, precious dogs, and hunting companions enter the frame.

■ OTHER ACCESSORIES

Various and sundry other accessories can round out the upland hunter's kit, but in most cases, they are specific to a certain style of hunting. Several companies make a belt festooned with pouches for upland use. These offer storage for birds and shells, and often water or other needs. They are light, efficient, and great in the quail fields or woodcock bottoms. Unfortunately, they do not provide enough surface area for the effective application of orange, and should therefore be worn in complement to an orange shirt or jacket.

Cartridge bags or speed bags are essential for driven shoots, where high-volume shooting requires a plentitude of shells. This piece of equipment fits in with the continental or driven bird aesthetic, and will be fleshed out in greater detail in a later chapter.

Finally, a soft but protected gun slip or case is a necessity when traveling to the bird cover or between coverts. If you travel to hunt, carrying a hard-sided travel case into the field is an unequivocal sign of being a novice; it should be avoided at all costs. A zippered, padded case or a similarly padded slip, or even a Teflon-impregnated gun sock, allows you to transport your intact gun from place to place without risking scratches or dents. In some states, however, a locked case is required for transport in a vehicle. If that is the situation, the hard case can remain in the vehicle, or a trigger lock, widely available at sporting-goods stores, will render a firearm legally safe in transit.

Where to Hunt

Chapter 6

Where to Hunt

In many ways, a discussion of where to hunt takes place once the logistical hurdles have been cleared, the legalities have been observed, and you, the newly minted upland hunter, are ready to take to the field. As I consider what guidelines I can offer regarding access and cover assessment, I am struck by the fact that this step—this physical entrée into wild places—is a significant milestone and one to be congratulated. By the same token, it is a step hard to advise upon in general terms, simply because access and cover can vary tremendously by region, species, and state regulation. I'll therefore speak to the common challenges, the common solutions, and the overarching considerations that might help you get out into the field with a gun in hand and some likelihood of seeing a shootable bird.

I must admit that with regard to my own early searches for a place to hunt, I got pretty lucky. Remember those benevolent teachers I mentioned earlier? Many of them were kind enough to share some pet spots with me, or at least direct

me toward the places that everybody knew about already, but nonetheless produced a bird or two each season. But the hand-holding only went so far; eventually I was nudged out of the nest, and encouraged to undertake what proved to be one of the more rewarding bits of hunting for me, namely scouting out my own spots.

When I started out hunting in northeastern Vermont, I was a hippie college kid in possession of a wobbly gun and a twenty-year-old car with cigarette burns in the upholstery. Gas was cheap, and the gravel roads that crisscrossed the Canadian border were widely unpatrolled, and nearly untraveled. As self-identified bird hunters, my buddies and I generally located good grouse habitat by driving around and looking for birds pecking gravel by the roadside. Where we saw such behavior, we tumbled out with guns and shells and wandered into the woods in pursuit. We were not road hunters per se,

as these places tangential to the gravel roads became our reliable coverts (note that grouse and woodcock hunters refer to their spots as such), and places we returned to year after year. We learned that grouse and poplar stands adjacent to young spruce or fir strips were synonymous, and we thereby learned to identify likely habitat empirically. Land was rarely posted, and hippie bird hunters were something of a novelty. The hill farmers and loggers more or less laughed off our very presence, reserving all of their disapproval and territoriality for the deer hunters. When we drove those same roads in the fall, apple trees bearing fruit were often visible on the hayfield and pasture edges, and these too were indicators of likely cover. Moist alder runs spelled woodcock, and alders were to be located in concert with streams and beaver meadows. We generally adhered to the adage that good grouse and woodcock cover is anything thick enough that a fellow can't throw a dead cat through it. The scouting that I did alongside my college friends was the result of some serious windshield time that spawned a growing understanding of the habits of our intended quarry.

Prior to that, and coincident to it, we spent an incredible amount of time wandering around in the woods. In and out of the bird season, we walked and snowshoed and skied and camped in the place we then called home, and we learned it well. Walking the woods with no clear intention sometimes brought about the thundering departure of a grouse or the twittering rise of a woodcock. We were operating on loose schedules back then, and the woodlands were our playground; by exploring them we learned the local topography and where the birds occurred, in what quantity, and in what season. This process of discovery was not methodical, or particularly intentional. It became central to our development as hunters, though, serving as an education and foundation for the hunting that would become more refined over time.

By virtue of the region and era in which I got started, my navigation of the "where to hunt" question, though undertaken honestly, was made fairly easy. But, unlike me, most aspiring hunters don't live in rural areas, don't belong to agricultural communities with laissez-faire attitudes toward bird hunters, and don't have the luxury of being nested within an educational environment focused on land use, wildlife, and conservation. For folks less fortunate than I, this question of where to hunt is honestly the most challenging obstacle facing a new upland hunter. Land access is the biggest issue, as trespassing laws, land-use parameters, and absentee landowners make matters of access quite blurry. But even where access is granted, evaluating cover can be monumentally confusing, and sometimes downright daunting. So how does a would-be hunter determine where and when to go, and what type of terrain offers some probability of success? This is where the onus of research falls upon the would-be upland hunter. Or does it?

The Preserve Option

In many areas, availability of public, huntable land is distinctly limited. The southeastern United States and the Texas ranchlands are both regions that are rich in hunting culture, but distinctly lacking in a public land base that holds populations of upland birds. In both of these places, and in truth across the country, aspiring hunters might well be served to simply attempt their first hunting forays on licensed shooting preserves. Time is a precious, and nonrenewable, resource. Though scouting bird cover and developing relationships that enable access can be rewarding processes on their own, many folks simply want to hunt. There is absolutely nothing wrong with this approach, and preserves remove the guesswork, making possible what can be a logistically challenging new activity. I would highly recommend that a new upland hunter locate

a preserve in his or her area, get a reference or two concerning the quality of the preserve from someone who has been there, and, if suitable, book a hunt. There will be birds; there will be dogs; there will be shots fired. On a preserve, you can rest assured that you'll be hunting with a fair probability of success right out of the gate.

A wide array of preserve options exist, depending on your needs and budget. The finest preserves offer shooting, guides, and accompanying dogs as good as any in the world. Many of these places manage thousands of acres specifically for bird habitat, and therefore attract and maintain populations of birds that will naturally reproduce within their cultivated habitat in addition to the birds that are supplemented. You'll pay for access to such ground, however. Companies such as Orvis make it a point to evaluate and recommend preserves and lodges of top quality, and such recommendations can be invaluable. An Orvis endorsement establishes that birds fly high and hard, guides are professional, cover is natural and expansive, and dog work is first-rate. Nothing is worse than a paid-for hunt in which the birds refuse to fly and the guide runs only dogs hell-bent on catching and killing every bird you've paid for. Again, invest wisely and you shall be rewarded.

Poorly run preserves are a travesty. The biggest issue with such operations is the propensity for birds that don't fly. When a preserve maintains birds in an enclosure where they cannot achieve flight condition or build a flushing response, and when those same birds are dizzied and shoved under a bush immediately preceding a hunt, things tend to go badly: pheasants and chukars refuse to flush, quails tend to "hop" or fly only a few feet at a time, and hunters are tempted to get their money's worth by taking low or unsafe shots. Well-taught hunters see the issues with such behavior both from an etiquette and a safety standpoint, but when money has been spent and a hunt has been long anticipated, decision-making can quickly devolve.

Hence the need for a suitable recommendation of, or a reference for, a sound preserve offering.

With regard to third-party references, however, hunters should never shy away from going straight to the source. Remember, a hunting preserve is in the business of providing a service, and you as a hunter represent a potential customer. Call the preserve and ask questions; establish your wants and desires. Remember, you are the consumer, and if a preserve operator refuses to talk to you straight, steer clear. The frustration and potential danger of a poor preserve hunt is simply not worth the hassle.

When planning a preserve hunt, be aware that you will likely encounter one of two pricing models. In the first, a hunter pays for a predetermined number of birds. In this situation, birds are generally stocked on the day of. That said, just because a field is seeded with ten birds does not mean that you, the hunter, will find and kill ten birds. Having spoken with countless preserve managers over the years, I have learned that by far the greatest source of customer service–centered angst is the prevalence of hunters who pay for a number of birds and fail to shoot them all. Remember in buying a predetermined number of birds that they will not be caged or forcibly kept in the bird field. Hence, you the hunter are buying based on faith, and hoping to see a high proportion of what was planted, but acknowledging that there are no guarantees. Hunting is, after all, an inherently unpredictable sport. On the other extreme, a hunter who purchases a number of birds may gratefully encounter more birds than were paid for. In this event, it is good to have a sense of what a surplus bird or two will cost. Preserve owners should offer a set price per additional bird shot, and you the hunter can be the governor of how much extra cash you are willing to shell out.

The other primary model is known as early release. In this model, birds are seeded into fields prior to the season and allowed to naturalize. Typically, a certain number of birds are stocked through the season to augment numbers, regardless of hunting pressure. In this scenario, birds are often given more time to assimilate and become strong fliers, though they can and will disperse into natural cover. These birds will behave much like wild birds, though they will occur in greater concentrations. Typically, preserves that operate on a release structure that simply keeps bird stocks regularly augmented are higher-priced propositions, but the quality of the hunt will be better. In these environments, pricing is typically based on a half- or full-day fee, or on a package-price number of birds, with additional birds charged à la carte.

Preserves of all sorts can be located by calling local gun or hunting shops, or simply doing some Internet research. In most cases, a suitable preserve hunt can be found within a few hours' drive from your home, often much closer, even when home is a metro center. Pheasant, chukar, and bobwhite quail will be the likely quarry, and guides and dogs will be made available at an additional cost. A half-day guided hunt, depending on the number of birds shot or released, will generally run a couple hundred dollars per hunter at the time of this writing. Guides and handlers should of course be tipped, as dog food, gas, and vet bills can get expensive.

When booking a preserve hunt, be certain to clarify the specifics and expectations prior to arrival. Clarify whether you will pay a flat fee, or pay only for the birds you shoot. Ascertain whether there is a swap-out program that allows you to take clean frozen birds in exchange for your fresh ones. Ask whether there are loaner shotguns available, whether there are gauge or action-type restrictions for allowable shotguns, and whether nontoxic shot is required. Finally, clarify what sort of licensure, if any, is necessary for a legal day's hunt. Again, there are some great mom-and-pop preserves out there, and the good ones should be open, honest, and clear about their services.

Public vs. Private Land

If preserves are not your style, or if the cost of a preserve hunt is prohibitive, you have the option to hunt on either public or private/non-preserve land. If you really dig into hunting, you will almost invariably decide to hunt wild birds at some point, just to get a flavor of what was, and remains, our common wealth. Wild birds are the richest and rarest of

treasures, and hunting them is a distinct privilege, and wonderfully a right. In terms of assessing cover and gaining access, it is valuable to break down huntable land into that which is public and that which is private. Each has a different protocol, and each can be researched in a different manner. Moreover, region dictates in large part what the available cover, quarry, and land-use system will be. Remembering my early forays in hunting, I can vouch that many scouting and cover-assessment strategies that work in the Northeast are useless in the Southwest. I'll therefore try to provide generalized strategies that might well serve any and all would-be hunters.

In areas where populations of wild birds are naturally occurring, hunters may have the option of choosing to hunt on private or public land. This does not necessarily mean that said hunter will only be in pursuit of wild birds. Many states, sporting clubs, and other similar groups stock birds to augment, or replace, wild populations. Pheasants are the most common bird to receive such treatment, and, in keeping with tradition, their presence in many regions hinges upon various stocking programs. Hunting on private or public land—in contrast to hunting on a preserve—is governed by state and federal law. Hence, state and federal seasons, gun laws, trespassing laws, and hunting licensure are implemented and enforced by game wardens and the local constabulary. Though this hunting is free save for the cost of a license, it requires a bit more legwork on the part of the hunter to ascertain what land belongs to whom, and what land is legal to hunt upon.

■ PRIVATE LAND ACCESS

What I refer to as private land is privately owned by an individual, group, or corporation. In this circumstance, the land is managed according to the wants of the owner, though governmental regulations apply. Preserves occur on private lands, as do some pieces of truly monumental game bird

habitat not specifically intended as such. That said, preserves are licensed by the state, and therefore follow a specialized, and state-mandated, series of regulations. Other pieces of private land, either intentionally or incidentally, simply hold birds, due in large part to cover and land use. That said, a hunter cannot walk onto any piece of private land in sight and start hunting.

Trespassing laws vary from state to state. In New England, "POSTED" signs indicate that hunters are not welcome without express permission of the landowner, but strict laws dictate the parameters of legal "posting." These signs must be replaced regularly, spaced within a minimum frequency, and signed by the landowner. Private land that is not posted, or land that is not posted in accordance with state regulation, is freely accessed by hunters, provided that hunting laws are followed (though hunters can still be asked to leave the property). In parts of the West, matters are far different; often, the onus is on the hunter to determine what is private and what is not. And I would hate to see what might happen to a hunter who starts shooting the birds of a Wyoming cattleman without due invitation.

It can be quite difficult to determine who owns a section of private land. Often, town records will illuminate such details, as will some basic Internet sleuthing. When a landowner is identified, a knock on the door, a call, or even a written note can be of use in initiating a conversation about land access. I long believed in the knock-on-the-door approach, and I still do philosophically, particularly in rural areas. That said, I have recently experienced several encounters with disgruntled landowners unappreciative of my presence in their dooryard. This animosity left me cold. I still believe in the face-to-face, humble request for access. I'm more inclined now, however, to look for an avenue of introduction, or to place a call wherein I ask if I might drop by to discuss the possibility of doing some hunting on their backfields. If the cold call at a front door still seems the logical route, it may be a good option to arrive outside of hunting season. By initiating the conversation over the phone or by letter, or by doing so independent of the "charged" season, the loaded encounter is avoided and the potential for access increased. This can be a slow process, and something of a hit-or-miss approach, but it can also be extremely rewarding.

Once the conversation has been entered, be forthright and honest. Express that you wish to hunt birds on the property, and that you will be extremely respectful of the land. Promise to not leave spent shells on the ground, or cigarette butts, or candy wrappers. Promise to close any gates or fences that you open, and to be respectful of livestock. Offer to leave some birds for the landowner, if you happen to get lucky. Do some reconnaissance, and decide if offering a twelve pack by way of thanks would be appropriate, or whether a different gesture of appreciation would be warranted. Clarify that you will not harm any crops, or, better yet, ask how best to move through the land to pose minimal impact. Basically, be assertive in indicating your desire to abide by the landowner's wishes. And if you get refused, never *ever* push back; it's a battle that will cause more harm than good, for you and your fellow hunters. Simply offer a respectful thanks, and mention that if things change in the future, you'd welcome the opportunity to hunt the property.

My friend Pat Berry, the former commissioner of the Vermont Department of Fish and Wildlife, offers an additional tip. He often presents a landowner with a written code of ethics that he promises to follow when hunting their land, alongside contact information and descriptors of his vehicle. Such an up-front show of integrity can often tip the balance in your favor where access is concerned.

In the same conversation, there are several topics to avoid: don't try to talk farming, forestry, or land use if you are not *very* well versed in the subjects. Your credibility will be called into question right off if indeed you don't know the difference between corn silage and corn syrup, and that too will hurt your chances for access. On the flip side, genuine interest in land-use practice can be a great entrée into conversation. If you ask how long the family has owned dairy cows, or how one chooses to grow peanuts instead of soybeans, or how many generations of the family have been on the property, your humble interest might well be appreciated. Again, remember that private land holding birds is a hugely valuable commodity, and your gestures of goodwill could make a wealth of hunting available to you.

In some states, private landowners are incentivized to allow recreational access to land.

These programs are often geared toward sporting endeavors, namely hunting, and the approval of access is rewarded with a tax benefit. In states such as Washington, private land is also made accessible by reservation through the Department of Fish and Wildlife. Departmental websites can be a great source of information regarding special programs, and the lesser-known opportunities for access on some truly spectacular private land.

PUBLIC LAND ACCESS

Unlike private land, public land is governed and maintained as a benefit of citizenship, and it represents, once again, our common wealth. National forest, state forest, Bureau of Land Management lands, and state wildlife management areas are examples of publicly owned huntable lands spread across the nation. Many of these lands encompass hundreds of thousands of acres, much of which is legally hunted, but not all of which represents likely bird cover. Wildlife management areas are just that, and are geared toward providing habitat for game species. That said, these areas may be managed specifically for big game rather than birds.

An invaluable tool in researching access to public land, and in researching areas of likely habitat, is the good old state *Gazetteer* by Delorme Atlas. These bound atlases are available for each state, and they provide sound topographical information including elevations, roads, and waterways. More importantly for us, however, they provide clear delineation of public lands, featuring little icons of shooters in places where hunter access is encouraged. If state stocking programs are in place, or if extensive habitat management is a component of the state or federal program for the area, these specified access points are where such management takes place. Cross-reference with officials at the state's Department of Fish and Wildlife or national forest or BLM agencies, and you are potentially into some great public cover.

Where Might I Find the Birds?

THE HUMANISTIC APPROACH

So with access granted, the next step is to crank up the degree of magnification, and isolate likely game bird holding places within that accessed land. To elaborate on the ecology of cover types, the variances of cover by region, or the specifics of game bird habitat requirements by species would call for a comprehensive volume on its own. Moreover, to define, by state, land-access policies or preferences would prove exhaustive too, and hard to decipher. So instead, I'll offer my best underlying recommendations, and flesh out specific details where suitable.

By nature, or perhaps by an innate laziness, I rely heavily upon the people around me for help in most matters. Nowhere is this more true than in my hunting, both in the early years and now. I am tireless, and shameless, in the questions I will ask. This brashness, or perhaps humility, has gained me more access than any other piece of legwork. Remember back in the introduction to this book, when I related that what we novice hunters so often lack is that "country uncle," that mentor and guide who breaks our trail into the uplands? At the root of that mythic relationship is just that: a relationship. An education in hunting is founded in large part upon relationship and communication. Granted, upland hunting can be a wonderfully solitary sport, filled with silence and communion with the natural world. But education in hunting is best facilitated by others.

With the shifting identity toward becoming a hunter, with the assumption of certain skills and gear, with the assimilation of language and understanding of birds and guns and the upland tradition, you have become armed with knowledge. With this knowledge, you can ask the finest kind of question, namely the *informed* question, posed with purpose and intention. This too is a powerful piece of the educational process, and one that builds those much longed-for relationships.

But what is the question, and who should be asked? This is where I have some very direct experience to speak from. When I was starting out, I asked upland hunting questions of anyone and everyone who seemed to know more than I did. I asked questions on all sorts of subjects about hunting, but foremost I asked where to go. Hunters rarely like to hand over coveted coverts or secret spots to strangers. But my cynical self believes that hunters also love to be "in the know," and they'll sometimes prove their superiority by waxing eloquent about huntable places near and far. My better self believes that, when asked humbly, in a manner that expresses some understanding of the mystique of the uplands, one hunter will smile upon his aspiring brethren. After all, there is no harm in asking.

But who and how to ask? Let me pose some scenarios: if you've studied up on guns, you likely know of a gun shop or two in your area, or relatively nearby an area you'd potentially like to hunt. If that gun shop carries primarily assault rifles, they likely don't cater too heavily to an upland-hunting crowd. But if that gun shop has a gray-muzzled lab asleep on the floor and some ratty mounts of bobwhite quail on the wall, chances are that the old codger behind the register knows a thing or two about where to hunt birds. It can be daunting, and incredibly humbling, to walk up to the counter and strike up a conversation about what upland options lie in the vicinity. You may feel foolish, or judged, or condescended to in the ensuing Q&A. But I can almost guarantee that you will leave the conversation with some direction. After all, the codger wants to sell guns, and here he is with a hot new prospect in his shop. If he's sane, he'll give you just enough intel to afford you some success, and he'll hope to be selling you a new over/under shotgun inside of the New Year.

But how do you ask the question? My advice: put your ego on the shelf and just ask. "Hi, my name is Joe, and I'm just getting into upland hunting. Any way you could offer me some suggestions on where to go look for pheasants? I'm kind of going about this without much help . . . " That ought to work. And if it doesn't, call another shop, or a shooting range, or an officer at the state's Department of Fish and Game. If you have a friend who mentioned in passing that his father-in-law used to hunt birds in the western part of the state, get that father-in-law's phone number and call. See a woman in the dog park putting a blaze orange electronic collar on a trim English setter? Saunter over and ask her if the dog hunts, and move forward from there. She and her husband go north every weekend for grouse—where do they go? What towns are good? How do they get access? In general, these conversations will open the doors, inform your journey, and get you on the ground in some cover that may hold birds. So too, it may enable you to build relationships, and learn what you can from the folks who have walked the path before.

What's more, don't undervalue the state and federal agencies, which, like the birds themselves, are part of our common wealth. A little digging on state Department of Fish and Wildlife, Forest Service, and Bureau of Land Management websites—not to mention the sites of conservation groups such as Ruffed Grouse Society, Pheasants Forever/ Quail Forever, and The Wilderness Society—will turn up contact info. Call, express your needs, and follow leads. I'm a huge believer in the power of the informed question, and it has surely served my hunting and my opportunities for access.

With all of this in mind, I might sound negative in admitting that intel regarding upland bird cover is tough to attain from others. For one, not many people hunt birds in earnest, compared to those who hunt big game or waterfowl. Bird cover is therefore hard won, and not easily given. Perhaps the best allies in the fact-finding process are deer hunters and trackers, as they cover more ground than most sportsmen, encounter birds aplenty due to their stealth, and generally don't care if the bird populations see some losses. Befriend a deer hunter and you may find a steady stream of information.

■ THE ACADEMIC APPROACH

When considering non-preserve options, the discussion of where to hunt quickly becomes a chicken-or-egg question (pardon the pun). Likely bird habitat is known as cover, and there is no need to consider how best to access a piece of private land if that private land holds no likely cover or birds. Conversely, without gaining access, you may never know what lies beyond that fence, over that ridge, or in that canyon by way of cover. This is where a general understanding of species and natural history comes into play.

It is my firm opinion that a hunter should spend some time learning about his or her intended quarry. If you are to make the investment in a firearm, a hunter's safety course, and a new vest and chaps, you should invest equally in your knowledge of the birds. This process will not only heighten your connection to the landscape through which you will be moving, but also serve to make your forays afield far more successful. A sound first step in this process is to figure out what species you will be targeting. If more than one species is available in the region you intend to hunt, all the better. In my region, grouse and woodcock are often hunted in tandem, as their habitat needs can overlap. I know this because I've read an awful lot about grouse and woodcock habitat needs, desired cover types, and preferred food sources. I know that grouse like poplar buds and mast, and I therefore learned to identify poplar stands both in and out of foliage. I know that moist alder bottoms lure woodcock, as do the sweet soils of scrubby pasture edges. I know that the transition zones between the two—namely the successional edge cover that features young birch, poplar, the odd pine, bittersweet, thorn apple, and wild grape—are prime habitat for both species. I learned these things the old-fashioned way, initially academically and then empirically. I read up on cover, learned to identify it, and then walked through it. On occasion, birds were there, thus proving my research. But on a deeper level, this process enabled me a richer communion with and understanding of our landscape. I found birds because I learned where to look, which was truly empowering. I like to say that hunting took me to places I'd have never otherwise gone. Undoubtedly, hunting made me a far better naturalist.

So once you have a general sense of where to go to access birds, refine your focus by picking apart that landscape. In a given piece of national forest in Arizona that the Phoenix gun-shop owner turned you on to, you may see open saguaro desert and a hilly scrub-oak section near a windmill. Your research on desert quail guides you toward the moisture and oak cover, where indeed you find birds. Hunting Montana sharptails? Walk the knee-high grasslands, preferably in the company of a hard-running dog. The academic approach to hunting affords you a finer focus on habitat and cover, and puts you onto birds. The humanistic approach, however, might land you a by-god teacher, a person who has been there and is willing to show you the ropes. A combination of the two may best ensure that no stone is left unturned.

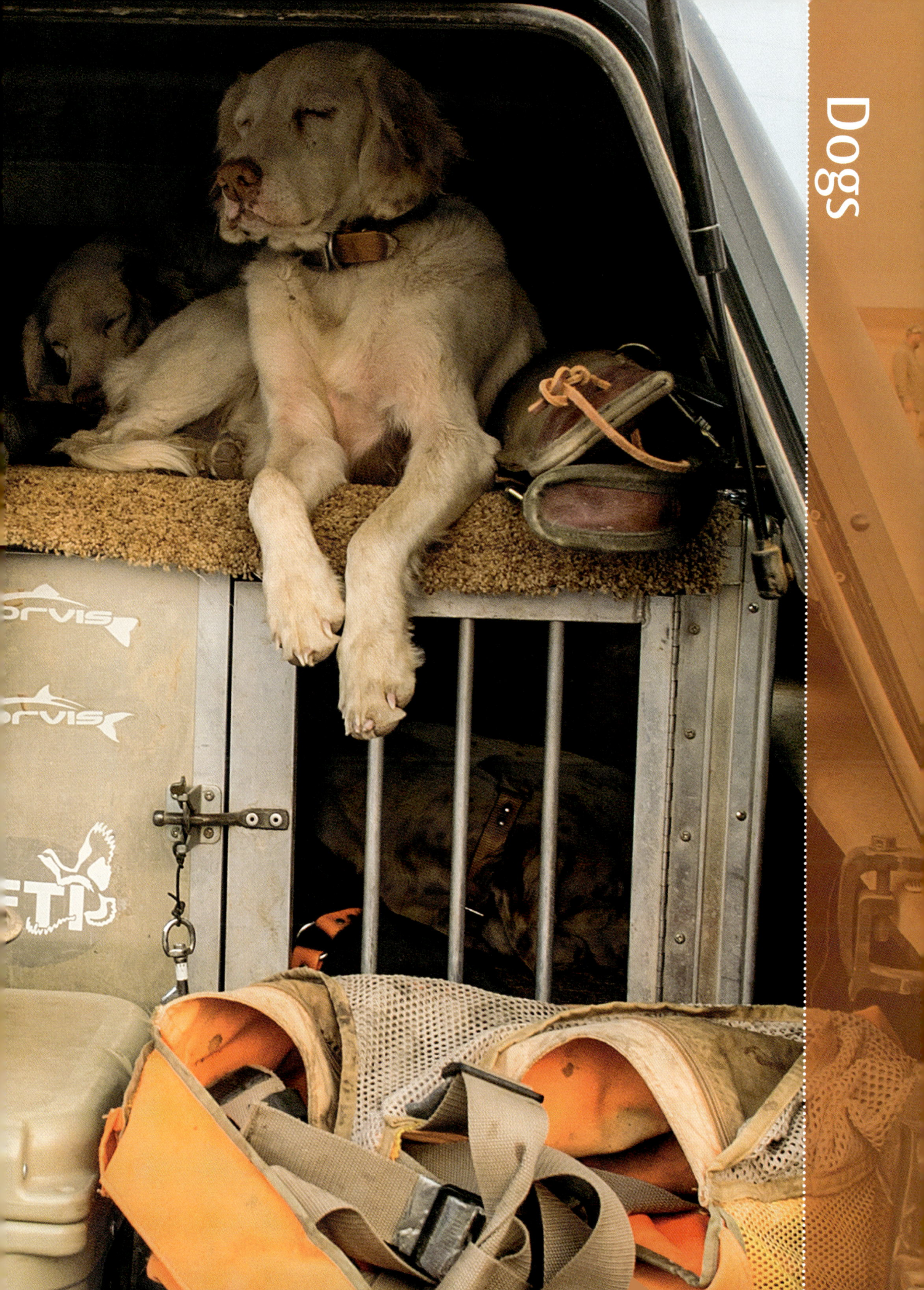

Dogs

 Chapter 7

Dogs

If you hunt birds for any amount of time, you will quickly see that dogs are so thoroughly entwined in the upland aesthetic that many would forego hunting altogether if dogs were not part of the picture. Orvis's resident expert and Field Trial Hall-of-Famer Jerry Ray Cacchio told me recently that he has been blessed in his life to have finally outgrown the need to kill birds, but his passion for watching a dog work a field has only grown stronger over the years. You will hear this sentiment time and again: dogs are integral to the upland experience, to the point that pulling the trigger becomes secondary.

You may, like me, begin hunting without a dog, and you may earn your stripes, and build some memories, being your own flusher and retriever. That said, once you finally hunt over a decent dog you'll see upland hunting for all it can be, and you'll have trouble going back to your dog-less days.

Volumes have been written about sporting dogs, from their training to breeding to the role of dogs in sporting art. For our purposes, this chapter serves as a relevant primer and a concise overview of what you need to know to enter the field safely, intelligently, and effectively in the company of a trained, purpose-specific bird dog.

Right off the bat, there are some designations that need to be clarified. Among the sporting breeds used for birds, there are three primary categories, namely pointers, flushers, and retrievers. Note that you will likely encounter both pointing and flushing dogs over the course of a lifetime in the uplands, and possibly the two in tandem. Retrievers present a bit of a gray area, in that true retrievers are trained solely for retrieving, but retrieving breeds such as Labradors are often also used as upland flushers. In this respect, breeds can serve multiple purposes, and designation of sporting breeds becomes an issue of semantics more than practicality.

The late Robert F. Jones, a noted and beloved hunting writer, claimed that his Jack Russell terrier performed admirably as a grouse dog in local Vermont coverts. A local fellow named Greg

Hagerman successfully hunts over a pointing rottweiler named Bella. It is true that a variety of breeds have been used over the years in the pursuit of upland birds. That said, several breeds have been developed over centuries, even millennia, to maximize either a point or a flush inclination. You may be familiar with these breeds on a colloquial level, and you may have even seen a few in your daily wanderings, but you may never have seen either type at work in the field. Many storied sporting breeds have also been bred away from field traits to exhibit standard show or bench traits, and the field bloodline may represent a far different beast than the creature you've seen in the dog park.

By definition, a pointing dog is bred and trained to freeze upon intersection with bird scent, ideally "pointing" or indicating where the bird scent is emanating from. This pointing refinement is simply an interruption of the pounce instinct, a trained-in delay of the natural inclination to make a grab at prey. A flusher, by contrast, works the field in tight quartering casts, zigging and zagging near enough to the hunter that when a bird is flushed, or put into flight, the hunter is within range of a shot. Both pointers and flushers can be trained to retrieve downed birds, but generally, the addition of a retrieve refinement is supplemental to the more pertinent find/point/flush. Different commands, different training, and a resultant different behavioral result applies to pointing dogs than to flushing dogs, and hunting behind one can be quite different than hunting behind the other.

At some point, you may decide you would like to explore the possibility of owning, training, and working a dog. Prior to making this significant step, I'd encourage you to hunt over as many dogs as possible, and alongside as many dog handlers as possible. In doing so, and in building this understanding of dogs at work, there are several key elements to be aware of.

The process of training and working a dog to effect is one that lasts for the entire life of a dog. It

requires of an owner or handler unique dedication and commitment, and invariably dog handlers, trainers, and guides build profound partnerships with their dogs. Seasoned dog handlers know their dogs' habits and tendencies far better than you ever will, and they will serve as an interpreter of sorts during the course of your hunting experience. When hunting with a dog and a dog handler for the first time, it is important to remember, first and foremost, that a hunting dog is a prize and a valued partner and family member of its owner. Hunting dogs are put in harm's way whenever they are put on the ground, and eager hunters bearing arms present a very real danger. Only personal safety and good judgment can keep dogs—and people for that matter—safe in the field. Nonetheless, bird dogs are shot and killed accidentally more often than any seasoned hunter cares to admit.

Shooting a dog is a cardinal sin, and one that is entirely avoidable. It is also worth noting that many lodges and guide services maintain a flat monetary penalty for killing a dog, and it can be a figure in the tens of thousands of dollars. When meeting a guide, handler, or dog owner for the first time, make certain to assuage any concerns by asking immediately how the handler would like you to act around his or her dogs. Would they like to be the one to flush the birds, or will their dog perform that task on command? Would they like you to walk with the gun's action open or closed? Would they like to direct your position in anticipation of each flush? By giving ownership of choreography to the handler, you communicate respect for the dogs and respect for safety. Having asked the question, you are obligated to comply with the wishes of the handler. It is an unspoken but overt reality that if a dog handler or guide feels that he, she, or the dogs are unsafe in your presence, they can and will call the hunt, kennel the dogs, and leave. Front-loading the dog conversation is a good entrée into a bigger safety conversation, and a fine way to express respect and willingness to learn.

Along these lines, remember that a hunting dog is a working animal. Certainly, you should *always* praise another person's dog, and you should be responsive if the dog swings by for a check-in and a cursory pat on the head. But once the dog is on the ground, the handler is the driver, and you should not give *any* commands to the dog or dogs whatsoever. Let the handler or owner receive retrieved birds, and do not pick a shot bird off the ground unless the dog handler indicates that you should do so. Every moment afield with a dog is also a training opportunity for that dog, and you'd hate to complicate the training sequence for the dog or the handler. Along similar lines, however, remember that even field-trial champions are imperfect, living creatures. They will make mistakes; they will break point; they will jump after birds. If you take a shot that is questionable under the assumption

that a seasoned dog will do nothing unexpected that might put it in harm's way, you will eventually be proven wrong. You'll never be looked down upon for holding off on a questionable shot when precious dogs are in the mix.

Pointing Breeds

As mentioned above, the role of a pointing dog is to intercept scent and then freeze. To see a good pointing dog in action is to see animation suspended; it's no surprise that the subject lends itself so readily to sculpture or works in paint. In general, pointing dogs will range ahead of the hunters in wide casts, working back and forth and side to side through the landscape. It is, for obvious reasons, best to work a pointing dog—or any gun dog—into the wind.

Over the years, selective breeding has refined bloodlines to a specific end, resulting in a loose difference between pointing dogs from field-trial stock and dogs from shooting or gun-dog stock. Field-trial dogs often run bigger and cover more ground than gun dogs, though this may be a generalization more than a rule. Field-trial dogs in open country may range well ahead of gunners, while close-working gun dogs in tight cover will generally stay close, but it all really comes down to the conditions, the cover, and the inclination of the dog.

So how close does the average pointing dog work? When the question of range comes up, I always think of a glorious day I spent with my friend Dan Michels hunting ptarmigan on the Alaskan tundra behind his English pointer, AK. The birds were plenty, the wind was strong, and the cover was wide open. Dan and I stopped to survey the magnitude of the landscape at one point, and to breathe in that arctic air, only to be hauled from our reverie by the realization that AK was nowhere to be seen. When Dan finally spotted him, a slash of white against the heather, AK was locked on point a good half mile away. Unfortunately, that dog was so staunch we had no choice but to start walking, though by the time we got to the point we were so tired I don't think we even got off a shot!

This little vignette illustrates how a pointing dog can and will stretch out in certain circumstances. Pointing dogs should work within the confines of the cover, and they should work within the range that their trainer or handler has mandated for them. Once on point, they should stay put. A dog in search of spooky grouse should hunt close to allow the hunter ready access to any points quickly. The same breed in search of tight-holding bobwhites beneath the Georgia pines can range bigger, as visibility is easy and the birds, once pinned, will likely sit tight while the hunters approach. A truly great pointing dog will shift his range with regard to the cover type, and will have the dexterity to hunt any bird, anywhere. All good pointing dogs are trained to be staunch, and will hold a point until released to reposition themselves.

Even open cover features enough low-lying brush that pointing dogs will disappear and reappear from visual contact through the course of a hunting day. For this reason, they are often fitted with mechanical beepers or bells. Bells are the more traditional locator, but they work in a slightly counterintuitive manner. What I mean to say is that a bell-wearing dog locked on point emanates an absence of sound, necessitating that the hunter keep track of the bell at all times, to be cognizant of the time and location where and when it goes silent. A beeper, on the other hand, often has a range mode and a point mode, enabling a moving dog to be tracked through thick cover, and a dog on point to be located by a different tone or cadence. The beeper is mechanical, and it interrupts the organic quality of the upland experience, but it also eliminates a vast range of headaches. I'm a sucker for tradition: I like beepers but use bells, and spend more time looking for my dog (and not shooting birds) than I should.

When approaching a dog on point, there are a few considerations to bear in mind. Though the dog may be nose to the ground and intent on a single patch of forest floor, it is never good to try to see what is on the ground ahead of the dog. Upland birds were designed over millennia to be hard to see against the landscape; your job as an upland hunter is not to disentangle that millennia of evolution from the surrounding cover. A pointing dog can smell what you cannot hope to see, so trust him and let him do his job.

A bird emanates a cone of scent that grows increasingly wider and less distinct as it disperses in a downwind direction. A dog will generally look up that scent cone and lock on point, repositioning on command to get a bigger and better nose full. What you as a hunter need to do is walk up that cone and flush the bird. There is, however, no exacting way to tell if the actual bird is two or twenty feet from the dog's nose. Therefore you must walk up the assumed scent cone with gun up and at the ready, with eyes taking in the aerial space before you and peripheral vision engaged. Trust that a bird will be there and that it will flush, and use your energy to get ready to do the job of shooting.

Occasionally, a flushing dog, walking at heel directly beside the handler, will be released to perform flushing duties. At other times, the handler or guide will walk ahead of pointing dogs and beat the brush, in order to flush birds on behalf of the gunners. Regardless of the process, be aware that when someone or something other than you is flushing, awareness of the scene is paramount. Be cautious, and be aware of the people and dogs all around you.

In the event that a bird does not flush, the pointing dog will be released from point by command, and will be allowed to reposition. This process can play itself out several times until the bird flushes, the scent goes cold, or the dog loses interest.

Standard pointing-dog training incorporates backing training for use when multiple dogs are working at once. Backing refers to the standard practice that when a dog goes on point, successive dogs—upon seeing that point—will similarly freeze and honor the initial point. This action ensures that successive dogs do not run over or disturb the bird pointed by the initial dog. A perfect tableau of two pointing dogs afield often features one dog locked on scent, and a second dog behind the first, locked in a backing point. It's quite an impressive thing to see in practice.

Pointing dogs come in all shapes and sizes, but there are a few usual suspects where breeds are concerned. Within each breed there are variations, which I'll speak to in brief. Certain breeds are more logically employed for certain tasks, but there are no hard-and-fast rules governing what breed for what bird or otherwise. All pointing breeds can point, can be taught to retrieve, and can hunt any species of upland game, though hard-running birds such as pheasants can make for a challenge. The only singular rule about breeds is that whatever breed you own is the best breed in the universe, and any hunting buddy who insults your dog is bound to be a hunting buddy no more. The following is a list of the most prominent pointing breeds seen in North America.

■ ENGLISH POINTER

English pointers are largish (forty- to sixty-pound) shorthaired pointing dogs. They are known for their stamina and strength, and the intensity with which they establish and hold a point. A full tail is a standard of the breed, and a stylish pointer will

hold his tail high and straight when on point, even when his nose and chest are near the ground. The common color scheme is dominant white with an overlying pattern of black, liver, lemon, or orange, or two in combination.

English pointers, often simply called pointers, are usual suspects in the field-trial finals. These dogs are incredibly athletic, and they can and will run big. They are favorites of open-country hunters where a "rangey" dog is an asset in covering ground and bird finding. They are iconic in quail covers, though they perform well across the disciplines, particularly in hot climates where a long coat can prove a deficit. Pointers are known to be gentle and sweet dogs, though their desire to hunt is paramount, and they need regular work to stay vital.

■ ENGLISH SETTER

English setters are the classic old-world gun dog. Though similar in build to English pointers, setters have a notably longer and more feathered coat. The setter moniker was given in deference to the breed's habit of lying down or setting when in the presence

of game. In a bygone era, this behavior enabled hunters and trappers to cast a net over whatever prey the dog was pointing, doing so without entangling the dog. English setters share dominant color schemes with pointers, though "ticking" and a bluish, roan hue can be common. The show lines of this breed are a far cry from the lithe and nimble field variants, almost to the point of being unrecognizably related.

English setters, like pointers, are athletic and big running, though they adapt well to tight cover. Being a widely favored breed throughout the heyday of North American upland hunting, they are often featured in classic sporting art. They are elegant dogs, though their long coat can prove a challenge in especially hot regions, or in areas where burrs, briars, and other impediments quickly become entangled in their coats.

▪ GORDON SETTER

The Gordon setter is an increasingly rare breed to see afield, as much of the bloodline has been steered

to highlight bench or show traits. That said, the field Gordon is similar in all manner to the English setter, but with a signature black and tan color scheme.

■ IRISH, RED, OR RED-AND-WHITE SETTER

The Irish lines of the ancestral setters featured a characteristic rich-red coat, either in total or in distinctive islands over an underlying white. These dogs were taken far from their sporting bloodlines in a breeding program intended to produce a bench or show standard, and much of the great Irish setter sporting genetics were lost. A recent resurgence in these breeds has seen a curated breeding program, and, though rare, the lighter-boned, trim, sleek Irish setters of yesteryear are returning to the uplands.

■ GERMAN SHORTHAIRED POINTER

Though somewhat similar in profile to the English pointer, GSPs (as they are often called) are bigger and more rugged on the whole than their English counterparts. GSPs are favored in the craggy uplands of the American West, where their longevity, stamina, versatility, and general hardiness are an asset. They are, in general, slightly less nimble than the English pointers or the setters, and, lacking a full tail, their point does not share the statuesque quality of the others. That said, GSPs are hard to beat where the terrain is steep, rocky, or otherwise less than hospitable to a more fragile pointing breed.

German shorthairs are typically liver in color, or liver and white, or solid with islands of liver ticked in white. Their coats are short and slick, and therefore easily maintained. They are, like most of the continental gun-dog breeds, avid retrievers, swimmers, and game trackers as well. When it comes to hunting down crippled birds, few pointing breeds can hold a candle to the GSP.

In loose terms, GSPs are great dogs for birds that tend to run, or for birds found in steep terrain. They are excellent chukar dogs, admirable pheasant dogs, and great on mountain birds such as forest grouse or mountain quail. You'll see this breed much in favor in the Mountain West, Northwest, and canyon country.

DOGS 145

■ **GERMAN WIREHAIRED POINTER, WIREHAIRED POINTING GRIFFON, AND DEUTSCH DRAHTHAAR**

Though the GSP devotees out there will be pained to hear me say so, these three breeds behave in a manner much similar to their shorter-haired cousin. As the name would imply, these breeds are a versatile, continental hunter characterized by a longish wiry coat over a dense undercoat, making them ideal harsh-condition dogs. Their coat protects them from cold and water, as well as physical impediments such as thorns and brush. All are festooned with a trademark beard.

As a very loose generalization, the Drahthaar is the most ruggedly muscular of the three, the Griffon is the longest haired, and the German wirehaired pointer is the most common, with the most refined bloodlines. All were developed to hunt furred game and birds, all can retrieve on land and water, and all have a developed knack for tracking crippled game.

■ AMERICAN AND FRENCH BRITTANY

The Brittany is a small (thirty- to forty-pound) continental gun dog often referred to as a "spaniel" due to a now-obsolete AKC denomination and an obvious genetic relationship to the spaniel lines. American Brittanys are sweet, biddable, and extremely nimble dogs that work well in close quarters or broken cover. The French line, whose members are often slightly smaller and identifiable by a black nose, is somewhat less common in the American uplands.

The American Brittany standard is a small dog with a docked tail and a coat not quite as long as the setter's. The predominate color scheme is islands of orange on a white background, though liver and white dogs do exist. French Brittanys are more frequently tricolored orange, liver, and white or orange, black, and white.

Those who own and work Brittanys are a peculiarly loyal lot (I count myself among them), with several iconic upland hunters in their ranks. Noted author and photographer Ben O. Williams runs a huge string of American Brittanys through his beloved Montana covers, and field-trial legend Delmar Smith is the man behind a line of dogs that remains, generations later, the envy

of many. Brittanys have been used to great effect in all cover types for all species, but they are likely most readily found in the grouse and woodcock woods of the Northeast and Upper Midwest or in the grasslands of the American West. They are sweet to a fault, and capable of adapting their style to the cover type as well as any pointing dog on the scene.

■ VIZSLA

The vizsla is an old-world breed with prominent origins in Hungary, and a historical record that dates back for centuries, if not millenia. The breed was favored as a sporting dog and a companion dog alike, and bloodlines were so revered by Hungarian aristocracy that the breed has remained intact and relatively unchanged throughout modern history.

After a widespread influx of GSPs and English pointers in the bird fields of Europe post-World War II, the vizsla faced near extinction. That said, the vizsla has waged a dramatic return to prominence and widespread recognition, and popularity in the United States has risen dramatically.

The vizsla bears a trademark golden-rust coat of short, coarse hair. They resemble an English pointer or a light-boned GSP in profile, though they are often confused with either Rhodesian ridgebacks or redbone coonhounds. In the field they are stylish and intent pointers, energetic game finders, and sound retrievers. Due to their relatively recent arrival on the American upland scene, they have yet to take a position of prominence as a breed in the field.

■ WEIMERANER

Photographer William Wegman can be credited with ensuring that the striking "Gray Ghost" has gained great popularity in recent years as a pet or companion breed. With origins in 19th-century Germany, the breed was developed to hunt all manner of game, from boar and stag to birds. It has since been refined into a more dedicated bird dog, with an equally dedicated following. It is an arresting silver-gray color, with a short sleek coat, regal bearing, and fine musculature. It looks very much like a silver vizsla with a docked tail.

Due to a fairly shallow gene pool and an overwhelming interest from nonsporting owners, the breed has lost some provenance as a hunting dog. That said, there are some great Weimeraners out there who perform admirably on all manner of tight-holding birds.

■ LESS-COMMON BREEDS

There are a myriad of other pointing breeds that I have not referred to in detail here, but that nonetheless are beloved or regionally specific. Several are wirehaired variants of the breeds listed above,

and several are old-world pointers found almost exclusively on the Continent. Still others, like the pointing Lab, represent flushing or retrieving breeds that have shown an anomalous tendency to point, a tendency that has been selected for and refined. All told, I have described the most common breeds encountered in the North American uplands, or in the historical record of bird hunting in North America. Hunt long enough and you will run into all of these breeds, though English setters, English pointers, and GSPs will be by far the most common.

Flushing Breeds

Flushing dogs are bred to work close ahead of advancing hunters, quartering side to side in the hope of intercepting scent. When the scent cone is crossed, rather than freezing, the flushing dog takes on a different attitude, with rapid tail movements and an apparent "birdiness" or intensity. Imagine that the scent cone is a vortex of sorts, and the flushing dog is impelled to work up the scent cone quickly, attempting to find the genesis of that great smell. Generally, the waiting bird doesn't look forward to this introduction, and it will depart, or flush, with great conviction. After the flush, a good flushing dog will sit as the shot is taken, and will pursue the shot bird only when released by the handler. Where whoa is the standard command for steadying a pointing dog, hup or a whistle blast should stop a flushing dog on a dime, and have him sitting tight until released.

Very few dogs are steady to a textbook degree, and hunters should be aware that flushing dogs can and frequently do jump after a flushing bird, occasionally catching one. Generally, caught birds are pen raised, with escape instincts and muscles somewhat less developed than those of their wild brethren. Shots taken over flushing dogs will be well earned and exciting, but great care should be taken that the bird has flushed well clear of the

dog, particularly in thick cover or where pen-raised birds are the intended quarry.

By virtue of the fact that the flushing dog's work should result in shots taken at reasonable range, the dog must work close to the hunters. Proper training, confident handling, and a sound genetic foundation should result in a dog that stays within range. Some would say it is the burden of the flushing dog hunter, however, to move quickly through the cover in pursuit of the dogs, and to essentially accommodate the dog's pace. What's more, the hunter that follows a flusher has to be prepared to get off a shot fairly quickly, and walking with your gun loaded and ready is more or

less a prerequisite. In some cases, well-trained flushers will negotiate a pace optimal for the advancing hunter.

In addition to the quick and sporty hunting that a flushing dog can make possible, the flushing breeds are great at tracking down and returning crippled game. The dedicated retrievers and retrieving breeds regularly perform double duty as upland flushers; in November you'll see the Dakota corn stubble teeming with long-legged Labs and some goldens as cock pheasants fill the sky. Even the smaller flushers regularly perform admirably on difficult retrieves and the dogged pursuit of wing-tipped or crippled birds.

The following is a list of the common flushing breeds seen in the North American uplands. This list includes two retrievers, namely Labs and goldens, as each are usual suspects in the uplands. Truth be told, many Labs never see the duck marshes at all, as they are so useful across the disciplines in the upland covers.

■ ENGLISH SPRINGER SPANIEL

Possibly the best known of the working spaniels, the English springer is among the most versatile of the gun dogs. The field line of springer spaniels was developed in the United Kingdom over the

last several centuries to "spring on" or give flight to (i.e., flush) both furred and feathered game. Initially, the flush was employed to make game visible to a waiting coursing hound or hawk, which in turn would catch and dispatch the quarry. As shotgunning became more refined, however, these springing dogs were put into service flushing birds ahead of an advancing gun. In this capacity, the retrieving refinement was made requisite, and single dogs were employed in finding, flushing, and retrieving shot birds.

With an arrival in North America in the early 1900s, the English springer fast became a favorite of the gentleman gunner. These dogs proved their versatility and handiness, loyally serving an owner in and out of the upland covers, and pulling double duty in the duck blind. Springers are driven and dedicated hunters, and incredibly keyed in on their handlers. A good one is a joy to see at work.

Though springers perform nobly across the disciplines, they are likely best used in the pheasant fields. Very few dogs can track and pin, and eventually flush, a pheasant with the athleticism of a springer. Springers also have their devotees in the grouse and woodcock woods, where their speed, agility, and scenting ability, combined with their propensity to hunt close, makes them an asset on spooky birds. Springers cross over wonderfully to the home, and they are sweet and eager family dogs. I'll admit that even I, a dedicated Brittany man, now have a wiry little springer wreaking havoc in my home.

ENGLISH COCKER SPANIEL

In the early evolution of the generic working spaniels in Britain, the litters were divided into two factions. The bigger dogs were set aside for work pushing and retrieving driven pheasants, as well as walk-up hunting a variety of game. The smaller littermates, on the other hand, were specified for work in the woodcock covers. Over time, with greater segregation of genetics and breeding, the English cocker became its own entity, and its provenance as a woodcock dog remains noteworthy, particularly in the United Kingdom.

With arrival in North America, an upland hunter following an English cocker found himself in the company of a little spitfire. These dogs quarter like a springer but on shorter legs, and they seem nearly tireless. They are remarkably dexterous retrievers, and true athletes, though they are lovable household dogs as well. They have recently come into favor when used in tandem with pointing dogs, as they can perform flushing duties in

the preserve environment to great effect. Historically, preserve birds were pointed and the dog handler was put into service flushing a covey of reluctant quail, or less-than-sporty pheasants, and his proximity to the flush created a dangerous situation. The addition of a cocker allowed the handler to stay out of potential shooting lanes, and also served to instigate higher, more enthusiastic flushes. If you hunt quail on a Southern plantation you will likely see some great cockers in action, as they've become favored throughout the region.

■ BOYKIN SPANIEL

The Boykin spaniel is a true American adaptation, albeit bred with waterfowl and flushed-turkey shooting in mind. The development of the breed is a wonderful story in itself. Legend has it that on a Sunday morning in the early 1900s a smallish, stray spaniel befriended a banker named Alexander White. White, who encountered the dog while walking from his home to the First Presbyterian Church in Spartanburg, South Carolina, took a shining to it, and soon found that it had an aptitude for retrieving. He sent the dog to his hunting partner L. Whitaker Boykin for training. Boykin was an avid hunter, and an equally curious dog man, and he too found the little spaniel, who'd been named "Dumpy," to have some admirable traits. With successive breedings, and the input of an ongoing refinement of spaniel and retriever bloodlines, the Boykin spaniel was born.

Through much of its development, the Boykin was regarded primarily as a waterfowl dog, but as the biddability and athleticism of the breed was recognized, it was employed for use in the quail and dove fields. Now, like many flushers, it is seen as a utilitarian gun dog, though it remains somewhat regionally favored in the southeastern United States.

The Boykin looks like a sturdy cocker, and is often confused with one. The coat type can be somewhat variable across different bloodlines, but the color is almost exclusively deep liver or chocolate brown with little variation. A small white chest patch is common and acceptable within the breed standard.

■ LABRADOR RETRIEVER

Far and away the most recognizable of the sporting breeds, the Labrador retriever is by many accounts the most popular recognized dog breed in the world. Labs were developed over the past few hundred years, with the earliest record in Newfoundland, in the Canadian Maritimes. Due to the versatility, biddability, and ruggedness of the breed, Labs were employed in a variety of tasks on their island home, not the least of which was retrieving waterfowl. Though still considered by many to be a dedicated waterfowl dog, Labs have seen service in varied roles, and they have seen service across the globe as upland flushers. Today, Labs are a preferred flushing dog, often serving double duty as a waterfowl retriever in season.

Due to the commonality of the breed, and the diversity of genetics, certain bloodlines and breedings have been selected for use in the uplands, but in general terms, field Labs for upland use are lighter boned, longer legged, and less "clunky" than many of the household Labs seen in North American homes. Now that's not to say there aren't bruisers among the upland Labs seen throughout the world, but in general, the dogs you'll see in the bird fields are trim and compact and a far cry from the 110-pound couch potato asleep by your neighbor's fireplace.

As flushing dogs, Labs are dogged, steady hunters. Though they lack the sheer energy and focus of spaniels, Labs often have excellent noses, and they are strong enough and steady enough to

work all day. Depending on training and cover, Labs often rely on this nose to find scent organically, and few can compete with the methodical, somewhat frenetic style of a good springer or cocker. That said, those noses are well proven, and Labs shine in the pheasant fields of the Midwest and perform admirably on the mountain birds of the Mountain West, in large part because they are robust enough to access the remote covers.

Much has been made of the "pointing Lab" as a distinct subset of the hunting Labrador retrievers, and indeed the pointing trait has been selected in several bloodlines. When encountered, these points lack some of the intensity and style of those shown by the true pointing breeds. The pointing Lab instead is bred and trained to delay that pounce-and-flush inclination, and the resulting pause is a "point." There are several breeders in North America who specialize in pointing Labs.

The final issue of clarification I'd like to offer with regard to Labrador retrievers revolves around the concept of the English Lab. In and out of hunting circles you will hear much made of the English Lab, and often they will be described as having specific characteristics: boxy heads, wide and short muzzles, and compact bodies. In point of fact, English Labs are simply Labs from England, or at least Labs with immediate genetics going back to the United Kingdom. Sporting dog breeding in the United Kingdom is an ancient and extraordinarily exacting art, and the bloodlines of a true English hunting Lab will be rich in field champion ancestry. Due to culture, tradition, and various rules, Labrador bloodlines in the United Kingdom are heavily curated, and dogs lacking an exceptional pedigree are not bred, sold, or exported. Hence, a UK Lab may have any of a number of physical variations, but as a rule they will prove to be top-shelf gun dogs.

■ OTHER BREEDS

Many other designated breeds are used as flushers, and many nonsporting dogs have been put down

in the uplands to serve as flushing dogs without adequate training or intention. In simplest terms, flushing birds is likely what any dog in the world would love to spend an afternoon doing, but a select few are maximally qualified, through breeding and training, to do so.

Among other flushing dogs that may make a showing in the uplands, there are field spaniels, water spaniels, golden retrievers, and Welsh springer spaniels. Any and all of these breeds can produce exceptional gun dogs, but the English springer, English cocker, and Lab are far and away the most common.

A Few More Thoughts on Dogs

In my work at Orvis, I deal regularly with gun dogs, and their owners, handlers, breeders, and trainers. I have been fortunate to know some great dogs and some great dog lovers over the years, and there are more than a few birds I've brought to bag thanks solely to the work of a good bird dog. As I noted previously, dogs add something to the upland experience that becomes, for most hunters, essential. But it is critical to remember that dogs are fallible. Even the greatest dogs at times bust a bird, or break point, or fail to make good on a retrieve. Even the softest-mouthed dogs on occasion chew up a perfect cock pheasant, or do a bit more damage to the precious flesh than we'd like.

But bird dogs are guileless to a fault, and they should be appreciated for their commitment to our upland pursuits. Their dreams are filled with flushing birds, and their waking days are filled with the promise of scent. Bird dogs have run themselves to death on more than one hunter's behalf, and they live lives festooned with dangers such as rattlesnakes and barbed-wire fences and errant bird shot. It is our obligation as hunters to appreciate them, to respect their artistry and passion, and to acknowledge that no matter how good we get, we'll never know half as much about finding birds as they do.

Into the Field

Chapter 8

Into the Field

The process of moving into the field is cathartic and exhilarating. It is where the final pieces of the frame fill in, and it is in effect the gateway through which the actual process of becoming a hunter takes place. It is a special and transitional action step, but one complex with nuance.

There are lots of subtleties to being an upland hunter, including etiquette, field safety, guide/hunter relationships, and how best to act around a dog. An understanding of these subtleties is of tremendous benefit to the hunter, as it will lead to a seamless guided experience and to future invitations afield. Conversely, a breach of etiquette or safety can be a deal-breaker, and a misstep at the wrong time and place can be the end of a hunt, or even worse, the end of what would otherwise be a fruitful hunting relationship.

Presuming that the physical process of venturing into the field is a pivotal developmental step in any hunter's growth, Orvis has framed the experience as a learning opportunity. The Orvis field hunting specialty schools afford students the chance to follow an instructor from the classroom to the clays course to the field in a structured and controlled learning space. This opportunity is truly unique; it provides the student with that "country uncle" for a few days of dedicated mentorship, and allows for learning in a real-life, experiential setting. If you have a desire to accelerate the learning process, and cater it to your personal needs, then a formalized education in upland hunting may be a wonderful option.

Regardless of the path you take into the field for the first go-round, it is OK to acknowledge that, as in any new activity, mistakes *will* be made. The key is to remember that where guns and people and dogs are concerned, the margin for acceptable error is deeply minimized. An untaken shot, a rushed approach to a point that bumps a bird, or a clean miss may be mistakes, but they are safe mistakes. Low shots, ground shots, or gun barrels that cross

in line of a shooting partner are less mistakes than gestures of poor judgment, and these breaches should be regarded accordingly. These are the mistakes that kill people, or kill dogs, and no degree of excitement warrants that. A missed bird can be made up for; an injured companion or dog cannot. When the hunter goes afield, regardless of his or her level of experience, certain rules of the road *must* be observed.

To my way of thinking, the best way to attend to these rules and considerations is to consider a hypothetical day in the uplands, and to summarize the components thereof. Attended to in sequence, we can identify, and in turn clarify, all of the little bits and pieces that go into a day spent hunting in the uplands.

Prior Planning

When traveling to the field or hunting destination, prepare accordingly. For simplicity's sake, dress in your hunting gear to the degree that it is comfort-

able and logical, and have the remainder of your kit (boots, chaps, vest, etc.) near at hand upon your arrival. A kit bag or gear bag keeps necessities in order.

Keep a bag of "extras" in your hunting vehicle that includes clothing to accommodate those drenchings and blowouts that invariably happen. A spare of every layer can often save your bacon, or at least make for a more comfortable day.

Though travel may require that your gun be stored in a locking hard-sided case, a soft-sided case or gun slip is the standard choice for safe gun transport during the day afield. Such soft cases are less cumbersome than hard-sided cases, and they allow for the gun to be transported fully assembled, unlike trunk or take-down cases. Soft gun cases or silicone-impregnated fabric sleeves should be accompanied by trigger locks where state or regional mandate applies. If your guide, lodge, or preserve will be providing you with a gun, be certain that ammunition of proper gauge and shot size is similarly provided. If it is not, or if you

INTO THE FIELD   169

are hunting alone, double and triple check that ammunition of appropriate gauge, length, and shot size is packed in sufficient volume for the day.

If you are driving to the field with a hunting buddy, take a portion of the travel time to communicate to one another what your expectations for the day are. By drilling down details as concretely as possible, expectations will most likely be met. Establish how you'd like to set a pace through the field, how you'd like to attend to payment and tipping of the guide, how you'd like to divide birds at the day's end, etc. Address any insecurities or concerns you might have, and any expectations of your partner. By saying before the day, "Hey, John, I just want to be certain you feel comfortable telling me if I'm shooting low or outside of my clear shooting lane," you have fostered an honest and safe hunting relationship. This degree of forethought may sound unnatural, or overly analytical, but it will serve the success and pleasure of the day, and might well lay the groundwork for a long and fruitful hunting partnership.

Hunting is a dynamic physical activity, requiring the hunter to attend to personal needs. Most guided hunts will operate out of a truck or ATV that is as well stocked as a small convenience store, but you should nonetheless come to the day prepared. Every hunter should have a small kit bag ready for action. Packed in the bag should be an extra layer, a rain shell, and possibly a spare pair of ear plugs. Don't hesitate to bring a water bottle along and some favorite snacks. You might also determine, when hunting with a guide or at a preserve, whether snacks and drinks will be provided. Indicate any food allergies, and don't hesitate to express drink preferences.

In anticipation of the day afield, have a good breakfast and ensure that you are well hydrated. Particularly if you are hunting in cold or wet weather, all of the standard rules for success in the outdoors apply. Build a fire in your belly with a good breakfast, and you'll hunt warm all morn-

ing. Also, take pleasure in building your own rituals around eating habits; one of the great grouse hunters of yesteryear, namely Gorham Cross of my hometown of Wellesley, Massachusetts, purportedly always traveled with a big box of Hershey bars, which he'd both indulge in and dole out to the farm kids whose families offered him hunting rights. True or not, it makes for a heartwarming story, and speaks to the celebratory nature of a hunter's little pleasures.

Make preparations for dogs as well. If hunting over your own dogs, always maintain food, ample clean water, and a med kit in the vehicle. Dogs require as much or more care as hunters; though better adapted to the demands of the sport, they

put on far more miles than we humans.

When I go hunting, I typically try to have both lip balm and sunscreen in my kit bag. Particularly in open country where wind and sun are a constant, a little protection for the lips can be a godsend. Moreover, sun protection is as relevant when upland hunting as it is in every outdoor activity. An ounce of protection is worth a ton of cure where sun is concerned. I also recommend a small roll of toilet paper in a plastic bag, for obvious reasons. One should always carry a knife and a small first-aid kit if hunting alone. As groundbreaking mountaineer and noted outdoorsman Paul Petzoldt once said, "Prior planning prevents piss-poor performance." Hunt light, but hunt right.

Upland hunters, like all sportsmen, can be a superstitious lot. For fear of being overly optimistic, and thereby dousing all chances for success, I hesitate to recommend that hunters keep a cooler in the vehicle with plastic bags and ice, alongside a flask of something worth toasting with. When hunting alone, proper cooling and transport of birds in a chilled environment makes for a superior product on the table (hence the cooler and bags). The flask is for that day that just screams to be commemorated. Drinking before or while hunting is of course a no-no, but a celebratory dram can be a lovely punctuation mark for that first double on quail or that first limit of roosters. Obvious precautions apply.

The Meet-Up

So you have prepared accordingly and have your gear assembled. You had a bottle of water on the drive, and you welcomed the day with a hearty breakfast. The hunt is to begin officially with a meet-up at a preordained time and place. If hunting with a guide, this might be a component of the lodge or hunting preserve itinerary. In this case, you will have been instructed to meet a guide in front of the lodge or at the clubhouse with guns and gear ready for the day. If hunting wild birds with an independent guide or a new partner, the meet-up might take place at a gas station, rural general store, or road turnoff. Upland birds generally sleep in a bit, so unlike in waterfowl, turkey, or deer hunting, an early start is rarely necessitated. That said, if meeting a new partner or a guide for the first time, be punctual and prepared upon arrival. My friend, the beloved longtime Orvis gunsmith Jordan Smith, once told me that five minutes early is an hour late. Quite a bit goes into the assessment of a new hunting partner, and putting the best foot forward can only help to paint a positive self-portrait.

Guide introduction and first impressions occur in tandem with your arrival, or your guide's arrival. (Note: Despite my friendship with several exceptional female bird guides and dog handlers, for the sake of efficiency I will refer to a hypothetical guide in the masculine for the remainder of this section.) As noted above, initial impressions tend to stick. Rest assured that when you first meet a guide or new hunting partner, there is a degree of assessment that takes place. Where guides are concerned, a positive but honest first impression can make or break a day afield, and you can curry favor by navigating the meeting artfully. Though I hate to generalize, guides share a certain consistency of thought. Remember, through the hunting day, a guide puts himself and an assembly of beloved dogs into the presence of countless unknowns, and a litany of potential dangers. A guide doesn't know, at the day's beginning, whether you have the savvy to avoid shooting him, his dog, his truck, or his other client. He doesn't know if you will be able to get him out of the field if he falls and breaks a leg, and he doesn't know if you will blame him for any birds that you in fact miss. He will be assessing you from the start in an effort to gauge just how attentive he needs to be, as well as how best to meet your needs and create a wonderful hunting day. A guide's livelihood relies upon his ability to meet, or ideally exceed, your expectations, but his safety

relies largely upon your judgment and composure, over which he has little or no control. Assuage his concerns early, and he'll have more bandwidth for attending to your enjoyment of the day.

Introduce yourself and be clear and humble about your experience and your hopes. Again, and I can't stress this enough, *overcommunicate*. Ask for a game plan of the day. Ask about any aspect of the hunting experience that remains unclear to you. Make certain with your guide that you have the appropriate licensure for the area and species to be hunted. Be sure to clarify which species are in season, and what legal bag limits are. You'd hate to put yourself or your guide in the position that occurs when an out-of-season or protected bird is inadvertently shot. Unfortunately, under this circumstance your guide will be on the hook as much as you will, and his licensure as a professional may be at stake if you, his client, act outside of the law.

Any guide worth his salt will begin the hunting day with a safety talk, or in a case where it is logistically appropriate, a safety video. If this does not take place, or if no safety talk is offered, ask for one. What you want to know is how the guide wishes you to move through the field (gun open or closed, how to approach dogs, etc.), which shots are appropriate, and what potential hazards may await you.

The safety talk or willingness of the guide to present some parameters for behavior brings up an interesting point. As I've said above, the guide or new partner will no doubt be assessing you at the first meeting, but so too should you be assessing your guide. Even if you are new to the game, you should evaluate your guide with regard to his behavior, willingness to communicate, and clarity around safety concerns. If safety is not addressed immediately, or if the guide at any point doesn't seem in command of the hunt, then there is a problem. Most guides are great at sizing up their clients, and will choreograph the hunt to the degree that they think is necessary. Some guides are less skilled in these subtleties. You are the customer; ask for clarity, and demand clear direction. A guided

hunt is a service experience, and you the customer deserve impeccable service. If it is not offered, or if any element feels unsafe, you are well within your rights to call the day early, pay the due fee, and leave. Address reparations later.

When first meeting a guide or new hunting partner, *always* open your gun as soon as it leaves its case, and *never* point the muzzle even remotely toward a person or dog. These are cardinal rules. *Do not break them.*

In general, a box and a half of shells is sufficient for a full morning's preserve hunt. That said, don't hesitate to ask the guide if you should carry more, if he will have more on his person, or if you will be able to circle back to the truck for more rounds if need be.

As noted in the preceding section, at some point either during the meet-up or when you first get to the field, some number of dogs will likely be put on the ground. They will run around and "air out," and likely get suited up with electric collars or bells. It is fine to ask their names, and fine to

pat them on the head if they cruise by, but *never* feed them or give them commands of any kind. Bird dogs are on the job as soon as their feet hit the ground, and they will be under the sole command of the dog handler. You may indeed praise them and ask the guide about them, but do *not* try to assert command over them in any way. Your guide will appreciate your respect.

Let 'Em See You Shoot

Oftentimes when hunting at a lodge or preserve, a guided day will include a bit of clays shooting as a warm-up. If such an offer is made, by all means accept. If it is not, ask if it might be possible. A warm-up on clays, when offered by a guide, is not to be considered an evaluation of your shooting prowess. Much to the contrary, the guide or dog handler likely wants to see whether you handle a gun safely and assuredly. Though you may feel silly if you miss the targets that are presented, don't miss the true purpose of the exercise. Once again, safety and reciprocal confidence in the gun handlers around you is of utmost importance, and of utmost concern to guides and fellow hunters.

If hunting with a new partner, or if a warm-up

Load Up and Go

Once the dogs are down and the guide gives the OK, you can begin to move into the cover. Your guide will likely give you a line to walk beside or through the field or woods. You may be able to see the dogs working, or, in thick cover, you may simply hear their bells or range beepers.

Imperative as you move through cover is your spatial awareness. Always keep track of where hunting partners are, guides are, and dogs are in relation to you. You and your fellow hunter should be roughly even with each other, with the guide between you and slightly behind. Dogs will range in front. If ever you cannot see a guide or a companion, give a holler. "You there, John?" will be sufficient for you to pinpoint John's location, and you can alter your direction accordingly.

If hunting over pointing dogs, many guides

on clays is not plausible, be certain to take the time to overcommunicate about the status of your gun. Take the gun from its sleeve, break it open, and show your guide or buddy that it is empty. When recasing it, be certain to overtly show everyone that the gun's chamber is empty. If you follow this measure, you will inadvertently (or purposefully) get your partners to similarly show you that their guns are empty and safe.

SAFE SHOOTING ZONES

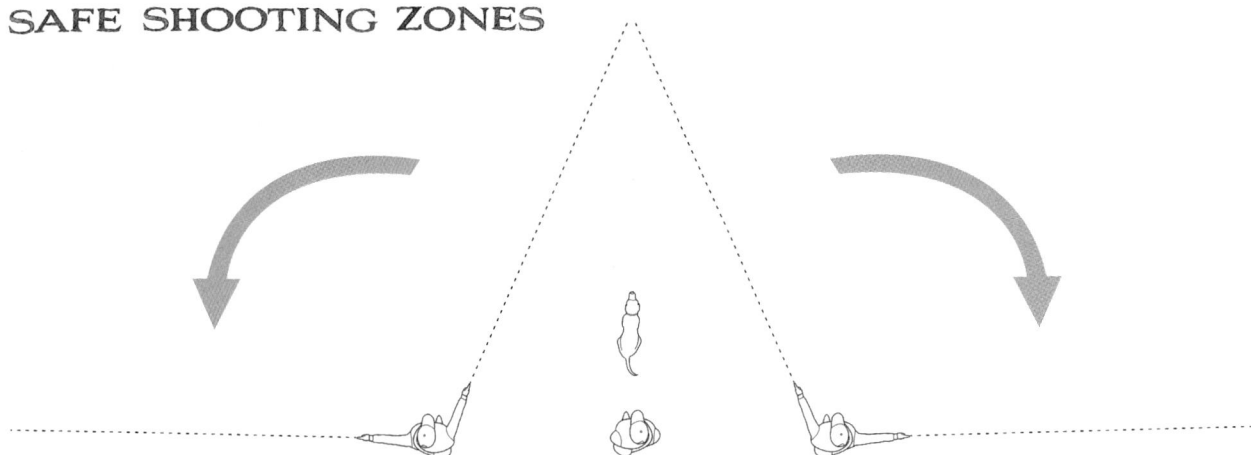

ask that guns be loaded (i.e., shells in the chambers), but carried open. Guns are ideally carried open either in the crook of the elbow, with the hand cupping the open action, or by the barrels with the action resting on the shoulder. Hence the beauty of a break-action gun. When a dog goes on point, the guide will position the shooters safely and appropriately. As you walk up to the point, close the gun and keep the muzzles aimed upward. Always the muzzles should point above the horizon and away from other people. Do *not* slide the safety into "fire" position until the bird or birds flush. Guides are great listeners, and they can hear the click of a safety slipping off from some distance; rest assured that your guide will be listening carefully for this sound. Keep the safety on and the muzzles up, and only shoot when birds clear the horizon or "level" mark.

When hunting with a flushing dog, or when hunting without a dog, hunters walk with guns closed. Some guides will allow a closed gun when hunting over pointers as well. It is a good move to ask your guide whether walking with a closed gun is permissible, and whether it is OK to shoot "wild flushes," namely birds that fly without having been pointed or concertedly flushed. If hunting over a flushing dog, or without a dog, all safe flushes within range should be considered acceptable to shoot.

When walking with a closed gun, always keep muzzles up and away from other hunters, with the safety on and the trigger finger outside the trigger guard. Two hands should be on a closed gun for safety and control. When you stop to change direction, rest, or reassess, open the gun immediately.

Generally speaking, a hunting party should be limited to two guns. There are of course exceptions to this standard, but two guns enable you to clarify shooting lanes nicely. Generally, the left-side shooter is responsible for covering any bird that flushes in his quadrant, and the right-side shooter covers any bird in his. Straightaway shots are a toss-up, but shooting obviously across the centerline is a breach of etiquette.

If a bird flies over you, or between you and your partner, or flushes wild behind you, always turn to the outside, with the muzzle to the sky. Turning toward the centerline creates a scenario wherein muzzles might swing across the guide or other hunters. Turn to the outside and take the shot if you can safely do so, but be aware of muzzle direction. Some handlers and partners would rather never shoot at birds that flush back toward the shooters. Clarify the comfort level about this contingency before the hunt.

In general, let close-flushing birds get out to a reasonable distance before shooting. When birds are shot at close quarters, the impact of the shot can, and often does, destroy the meat. Additionally, a short hesitation allows the shot spread to

open sufficiently to maximize margin for error. On a similar note, avoid any shot outside of reasonable range, namely beyond thirty to forty yards. Crippled birds are undesirable on multiple levels, and may well become lost birds.

If and when a bird flushes wild, call bird or mark in a loud, clear voice. This call will turn the attention of the party to the bird, and enable shooters to prepare. Moments are precious in the case of shooting at a wild flush, and your partners will be grateful for the heads-up.

When multiple birds flush in rapid sequence from a single location it is called a covey rise. A covey rise will seem like an easy opportunity for success due to the number of birds in the air, but they have proven the undoing of many an upland gunner. To add to your success, whenever a group of birds jumps together, concentrate on one. Once that bird has been shot and is falling, turn your attention to the next. "A bird in the hand," as the saying goes, is the first order of business, and successive birds can be attended to in time.

Bird Up, Bird Down

When a bird falls, mark its location. Birds sometimes fold and die immediately, but often they hit the ground with some life left, and proceed either

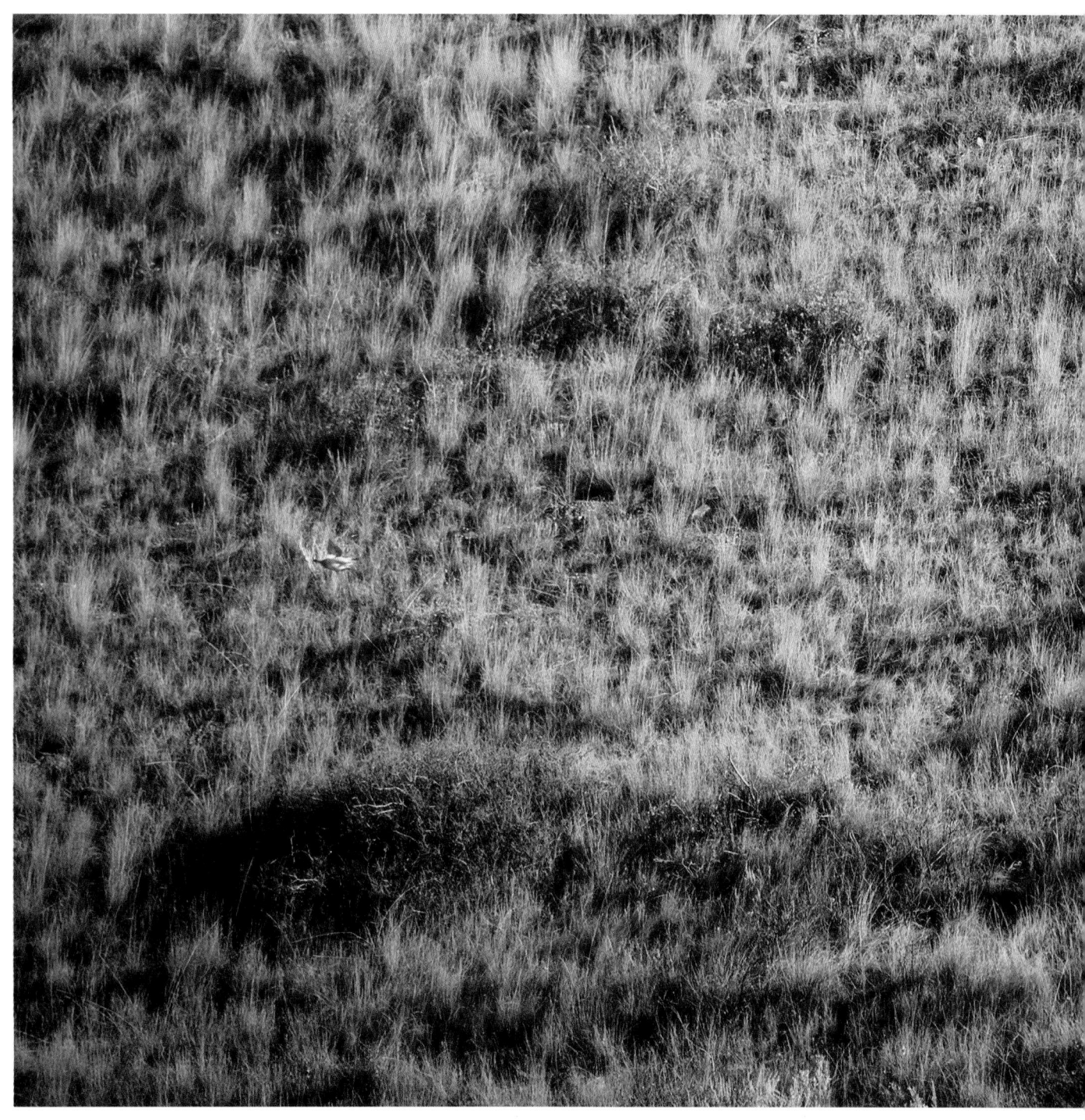

to run or jump and fly some more. If hunting with a dog, stay put after your shot, and maintain visual contact with the place where you think the bird is. If you are with a dog handler or guide, let the guide walk toward the downed bird while you maintain a visual mark on its location. You can direct best from your shooting location, so stay put and steer the guide and dog toward the bird. Marking downed birds is a critical element of sportsmanship, and regardless of whether you are in the company of a guide, it is the responsibility of the shooter.

If you drop a bird in tight cover, hang a bandanna or your orange hat on a branch near the position you shot from before going on a search for the bird. Invariably your sense of where the bird landed changes as your position changes, and it

can be nearly impossible to return to the shooting location after it has been abandoned. Marking this spot allows the shot to be replayed if you wish, which can prove the difference between a lost bird and a found bird.

When looking for a bird, particularly in tight cover, remember that a lifeless bird can get hung up in tree branches or brush, sometimes well off the ground. I remember vividly a short hunt I took on my way to work one morning, in a lovely little woodcock covert near my home at the time. My dog Sleeper pointed a woodcock, I shot and killed it at close range, and we proceeded to look frantically for the bird over the ensuing twenty minutes. Sleeper and I were nearing the point of giving up, and assuming that the bird had been

nothing more than a daydream, when something prompted me to look up. The lovely little bird was stone dead, caught in a thorny tangle just above eye level. Sleeper and I had maintained focus on the ground, and had missed the bird that was right in front of my face.

When looking for a downed bird, keep the gun open. Finish the task at hand before shooting at additional flushes. Conversely, if it has been sanctioned by guides and hunting partners, be prepared for additional shooting opportunities when a dog is making a retrieve on a downed bird. Often, in the singular pursuit of a retrieve, a dog will bust additional lay birds from the immediate area.

The Wrap-Up

After a successful day afield, you will be bush-whipped and tired, often windburned and muddy and a little bit tattered. You will also be elementally happy, even when the game bag is light. There are a few issues to attend to at the day's end, however, and they are delicate matters worthy of attention.

Most preserves or lodges have a preordained package price for a guided hunt and a given number of birds. Often, however, additional birds above and beyond this limit that are shot in the course of a hunt are attributed to a hunter's bill. Extra birds can be costly, and when birds are plenty and your aim is true, you can rack up quite a tally in short order. Make sure through the day that you reassess your bag, and that you clarify with your guide how additional birds will be priced.

Again, in a preserve environment, total bird count is of significance, primarily for financial reasons. A good pen-raised bird is not inexpensive to raise, or to transport, or to put in the field. If you and a partner shoot a goodly number and you are paying by the bird, have a clear understanding as to how the bag will be allocated before wallets come out. It is fine to pay only for the birds you shot, but it is also fine to simply split the total bill at the day's end. Either way, however, the plan should be clarified before a tense money moment comes to light between you and your shooting partner.

As in most guided situations, a tip is a given, albeit an unspoken one. In general, a tip for a guided day or morning follows the norms in the restaurant trade, with twenty percent or so being a standard. This tip is to be paid to the guide in cash, and should be prepared for in advance of the hunt, as the old "dig around in the pockets then shrug" routine does nothing to perpetuate future relations with the guide or handler.

One more note on tipping: though it may seem quite rational to do so, try to avoid asking a guide how much he should be tipped. In general, this question does little more than make the guide uncomfortable. Moreover, in asking this question, you run the plausible risk of getting a response far out of scale, and then you are in the complex position of either leaving the asked amount or shorting the guide what he expects. It's better to tip confidently, and perfectly fine to tip well, especially for an epic day. Bird guides are rarely wealthy, and you'd be amazed how deeply they rely on their tips.

Birds Down

For many years I lived on a ridgetop farm in central Massachusetts. The pastures and woodlots followed a few miles of dirt road, and in the encompassed acres I hunted grouse, woodcock, and pheasant. I did so typically in the frost of early mornings and the slanting sun of afternoons, and I did so largely alone, save for the company of a cocky little American Brittany.

These were the middle years of a hunter's life, wherein the frivolity of youth was giving way to a family and job that took precedent, and in turn I hunted around the edges of the day. Too often these edges were only fractions of an hour, but they nonetheless were mine. I even managed at times to find a bird or two.

On one such morning, in the tangled corner behind the Blackmers' dairy barn, I dumped a male woodcock just as the sun was cresting the hill. Being late for chores, I grabbed the little body and smoothed back the feathers, and admired it with the blend of joy and mild regret that I reserve for woodcock in particular. But with the sun rising and the day getting late, I tucked the bird into my game bag, whistled up the dog, and hustled back out of the covert to the truck. I scooted up the road to the home farm, pulled into the barnyard, and got out. I shucked off the vest and the whistle, and uncollared the dog. I threw the vest in a corner of the woodshop where its contained treasure would remain cool and shaded until the day's end. I then went off to see after a row of hungry Jersey cows, none of whom were too pleased with my tardiness.

I worked a full day in the October sunshine, ate dinner at the farm, and only when the stars were high did I return to the woodshed to pluck and clean my little bird. I opened the game bag to see the interior fabric painted with stark white droppings, the distressed leavings of a bird I'd assumed long dead; the woodcock had, after all, only been wounded. That bird had, at my hand, suffered the

indignity of a day spent crippled and forgotten, and undoubtedly in pain. It died slowly in the back of my vest. All of this on account of my haste.

I am not proud of this story. Truth be told, it is among the stories that I am least proud of in life, and it is not one I tell often or easily. It does, however, illustrate a point. The point is that hunters kill things, and they should do so with intention and with certainty. There is no judgment here, simply fact: if you set out to kill a game bird, kill it swiftly, and then do everything in your power to be certain it is dead. You owe a lovely creature at least that much.

This story, I hope anyway, pushes against a philosophical conundrum that is central to all hunting. We love these things we seek to kill, though we both protect and harm them, and feel a little bit sad about our compulsions. I don't know why this is. I do know, however, that an education in hunting is an education in purpose. It is also an education in absolutes. Perhaps this is what we stand to learn most through our journey into the uplands. I know that, in my case anyway, hunting has forced me to lean into nature's questions and nature's uncomfortable answers. It has shared teachings about finality, and taking responsibility for what you can't undo, what you can't put back. Hunting is not a catch-and-release sport.

It is no mystery that upland hunting, when done to success, removes a bit of flesh and feather from the living landscape. Hunting cannot easily exist independent of killing, and that distinction should be clear. Hunting is more than a lovely walk in the woods with a fine old gun; it is by definition an anticipatory action, done with intention. When followed through, it encompasses killing things, plain and simple. As you begin to identify as a hunter, it is common to see yourself as a different creature altogether than the one you've been before: being a hunter requires conviction, and the inevitable reality that your hands will get bloody, and the creatures that you love will die.

So where do we go with this conversation? The answer is too personal to address in specifics, but from a spiritual or philosophical standpoint, I'd offer one simple piece of advice, maybe better defined as a request: I'd ask that in becoming an upland hunter, you not forget to thank the birds that allow you that identity. I'd also ask that you read on, in an effort to ensure that your birds are killed quickly and efficiently, and with absolute certainty.

Use Enough Gun

One of the finest writers, sporting or otherwise, of the twentieth century was a gentleman by the name of Robert C. Ruark. In writing about his early adventures on safari in Africa, Ruark gained some notoriety for exploring at length the premise of "using enough gun," that is to say, making certain that a gun of sufficient caliber be used to effectively

kill what was often quite dangerous game. But there was more than practicality and safety to Ruark's assertion that a hunter should always use enough gun. To Ruark's way of thinking, and to mine, it is only fair and ethical hunting practice to be as efficient and effective as possible. Hence, handicapping oneself with insufficient firepower, insufficient shot size, or insufficient choke is antithetical to a sound hunting conduct. The same holds true whether hunting big cats or bobwhite quail.

In the chapter on guns, I trust I made clear that a twelve-gauge gun is not inherently more potent than a twenty gauge or smaller. Efficiency, ballistics, and personal comfort all play into a gun's end efficacy as a hunting tool. It is generally assumed, however, that longer shots and bigger birds require more gun, not because a bigger gauge is more powerful per se, but because a twelve-gauge gun, shooting at roughly equivalent ballistic performance to a comparable twenty or twenty-eight, throws more lethal pellets downrange, and therefore fills the air with more projectiles.

But what does this mean in usable terms? In essence, it means that the more lethal pellets that hit a bird in flight with killing efficiency, the more likely the bird will die cleanly. This end can be achieved with a greater margin for error with a larger-gauge gun. Conversely, when shooters handicap themselves significantly by shooting something as diminutive as a .410, the potential for crippling game is substantially increased. A .410 (which is a designation of caliber roughly equivalent to a sixty-eight gauge) throws a truly unimpressive pattern in conjunction with a relatively small shot and powder load at best, and therefore can't compete from an efficiency standard with its larger-gauged cousins. In a standard .410 round, there just aren't enough pellets involved to ensure a clean kill on anything more robust than a close-quarters quail or thin-skinned woodcock. Hence, as Ruark said, use enough gun. When in doubt, a larger gauge, loaded appropriately, will be more a blessing than a curse.

Shoot within Your Limits

Many novice hunters assume that two potential outcomes result from a shot-at bird: either the bird is hit and summarily crumples, or the bird flies away unscathed. Unfortunately, hunting is an inexact science. A long shot, or a poorly placed shot, or even a shot taken with insufficient choke, can sting a bird but allow it to carry off quite a bit of lead before eventually dying. The grim reality of hunting is that you, the upland hunter, will do harm. You will hit birds that you will not recover, and you will likely do so without ever realizing it. This is a reality of the experience.

As previously discussed, a shotgun hurls a little cloud of pellets into the future, and this cloud both disperses and loses energy with every foot traveled. It is the burden of the hunter to understand what sort of damage his shotgun can do, and what sort of performance he can command it to do. From a mechanical standpoint, and barring any obscene constrictions of choke, few birds are killed cleanly outside of forty yards in open cover, while most are killed far closer. This general rule of distance assumes that the hunter is using a suitable shot size, powder charge, and an adequate gauge of gun for the intended quarry.

But what does forty yards look like, and how do you apply split-second calculations in the field? Unfortunately, unlike in golf, a hunter does not have established markers with which to reference distance. The answer to gauging distance is practice. It is key that you as a hunter get comfortable assessing distances quickly, and making snap judgments about range. To do this well, you simply need to calibrate your eyes, and whatever estimating tool is wired into your brain.

To hone this skill, start looking at objects in space as theoretical targets. How far away is that fire hydrant? How far away is that shrub? How far away is the car from my front door? Start assessing these distances, and pacing them off. Likely, forty yards is farther than you'd think. Additionally, shoot, shoot, and shoot some more. Clay targets will give you an increasing confidence in your ability to gauge killing distance. In the end, though, only time in the field will ensure a suitable ability to calculate range. A Hail Mary shot at an eighty-yard target, even if the bird crumples, is less a gesture of heroism than of disrespect.

Cripples

Even if you are a crackerjack shot, you will at some point cripple a bird. By virtue of the mechanics of flight and the physics of shot pattern, in conjunction with the physiology of birds in general, a clean kill on a flying bird is the exception rather than the rule. Birds are more reptilian than mammalian, and as in all prehistoric species, their tenacity of life is impressive. Consider the stories about chickens with their heads cut off, and you'll realize that unless a pellet does structural skeletal damage, severely damages vital organs, or happens to penetrate what is a comparatively small brain and related nerve center, the bird will not die quickly. For this reason, you need to know how to manage crippled birds.

From a conservation standpoint, a dog is your greatest asset in locating downed or crippled birds. Regardless of whether a dog is trained to retrieve to hand or whether it will simply point dead, a decent dog will find birds that you alone will not. A cripple that hits the ground running will often only be brought to bag if a dog, trained to track down cripples, is on hand. Though it is impossible to quantify how many birds are lost in the absence of dogs, I'd venture it's a staggering number. Hunt with a dog when you can, if only from a conservation standpoint.

When a bird is shot, it may be dead upon retrieval, but often there is some nervous activity that remains. Sometimes too there is structural damage (i.e., a broken wing or legs) but no immediately fatal injury to the bird. In this case, as in any case, it is key to watch the bird fall and then mark its landing place, as it may not be there when you arrive. Moreover, follow your shots. Even if a bird flew off seemingly unscathed, it may well be flapping on the ground a few hundred yards up ahead. You'd be amazed how many birds fly off vigorously after a shot is taken, but fall stone dead a few hundred yards away. Follow up every shot, and give dogs ample time to search the vicinity before moving on. Haste makes waste in hunting, too.

If you find your bird alive, or if it is retrieved to you alive, there are several ways to dispatch it humanely. The most common method is to break its neck, and you will see guides and seasoned hunters alike grasping the head of a bird and swinging its body around in energetic circles. This can be effective or ineffective, but it is certainly indelicate. Often the head comes off altogether, which ensures that the bird is dead, but leaves a mess and a barbaric tableau. I'd suggest one of the following methods instead.

Option one: Grasp the bird by the body and rap the back of its head sharply against a hard object, whether a tree, rock, or gun barrel. This can be repeated if necessary until the neck goes limp. Often there will be some degree of nervous spasm through the body of the bird, but this response will subside quickly. If it does not, rap the head again.

Option two: If saving a bird for taxidermy, grasp it high on the breast under the wings, pinch hard, and hold. This process will suffocate the bird, but it will take a couple of minutes. It will, however, keep the body pristine for mounting, provided that the carcass is handled with care.

Option three: I personally carry in my vest a tool called a bird necker. These are commercially available through gun-dog and hunting supply retailers, and they are a nice tool to have when dispatching cripples. In essence, the necker is a pair of pliers that does not close all the way, so that a minimal space is left between the closed jaws. When a bird's neck is placed in the jaws and the handles squeezed, the vertebrae separate without the skin being broken, resulting in a swift, bloodless kill. Since my morning with the woodcock, I always ensure the demise of a bird that seems tenacious of life with my necking tool.

There are, of course, other ways to kill birds that are not immediately dead upon retrieval. Regardless of methodology, I encourage you to be confident and sure in your method for dispatching cripples. No creature is served by a waffling of conviction at the terminal moment. Do not simply assume that a bird will die quickly once placed in your game bag. Pick your method, kill the bird, and be certain about it. It is the due diligence of any hunter to do so.

Prepping Game Birds for the Table

Chapter 9

Prepping Game Birds for the Table

There are few delicacies more rare on the modern table than cuts of wild game. I'd venture that a mere sliver of the world's population knows the flavor of woodcock breast seared on the outside and blood rare in the middle. How many folks could possibly have tasted sharp-tail grouse, or mountain quail, or ptarmigan? All of these birds are remarkable as table fare, and all possess unique character on the plate. It is your job as a hunter to do them justice, and see that they are treated as the prizes they are. It is also your obligation to suspend your belief that all fowl should taste like grain-fed, battery-raised chickens.

Hunters and gourmands have differing tastes where game is concerned. For some, the "gamey" flavor that we hear referred to so often is simply any departure from the mild flavor of chicken, and, being different, is considered unpalatable. "Gaminess" or strength of flavor results from the diet of the given game bird, the handling of the bird once dead, and the span of time between the bird's demise and preparation for the table. All of these factors can add to the strength of the flavor, and with taste being what it is, I can't really venture a consistent recommendation as to how birds should be prepared. There are those who would prefer to keep the flavor of game birds as light as possible. There are others, like the River Cottage's famed chef Hugh Fearnley-Whittingstall, who would prefer a relatively heavy flavor. I cannot pass judgment on personal taste; I can, however, offer some insights.

The mildest-tasting birds have a diet rich in grains and mast or plant matter, and they have predominately pink flesh. These include quail, ruffed and blue grouse, chukar partridge, and pheasant primarily. Other species, depending on whether they have been pen raised, can be similarly mild in flavor and light in flesh color. The mildest game bird meat results from a bird that is shot, cleaned, and cooled quickly. The process of decay begins the minute a bird is killed. As time passes, this

process will increasingly tenderize the flesh of the bird by allowing enzymes the opportunity to break down connective tissue within the muscle, making the meat both easier to cut and easier to chew. Time and decay will also add to the strength of the flavor. When a bird is shot, there is no way to know what organs have been punctured internally, or what gastric juices or intestinal matter has been allowed to infiltrate the meat. Hence, to ensure a mild-flavored meat, I suggest the birds be cleaned and then cooled rapidly, and the flesh be rinsed of any potential contaminates.

The darker-fleshed birds such as woodcock, ptarmigan, and sharptail grouse have a flesh that is almost purplish and rich in flavor. These birds benefit from being treated a bit more like beef than chicken. Woodcock in particular have a livery flavor due in large part to their predominate diet of earthworms, which, I'd have to assume, taste a bit livery too. All birds develop deeper flavor when aged for a period of time (more on aging later in this chapter).

Field Dressing

There are those who say that it is best when dressing any animal to wear a pair of rubber or nitrile exam gloves to ensure that disease such as avian flu is not transmitted from the animal to the processor. Indeed, gloves make for a quick and easy cleanup, and they do provide an added precaution against communicable diseases or infections. That said, I'd be lying to claim that I wear gloves in processing my birds, though I know I should. Nonetheless, it is my duty here to encourage you to wear protective gloves when processing any wild game animal.

If mild-tasting birds are your preference, I'd recommend that your birds be field dressed immediately upon retrieval. This essentially means that innards be removed. To do so, hold the bird breast up in one hand, and determine where the sternum or breastbone ends. Remove feathers from the tip of the breastbone to the anal vent by plucking them sharply out of the skin. From there, make a shallow cut through the exposed skin and muscle, ensuring that you not cut so deep as to puncture the intestine. I perform this operation by taking a pinch of this soft skin and making a slice perpendicular to the breastbone, namely across the body. Once this cavity is open, reach in with a finger or two and pull what viscera you can down and out. The entire mass will be largely connected, and provided that the bulk is removed and the intestines are not torn, the vent can be cut free and the mass discarded. Once vacant, the body cavity can be stuffed with dry grass to accelerate cooling.

A lesser known but equally effective field-dressing method requires the use of a gut hook. This inelegant-sounding device is often seen on pocketknives built for bird hunters, though you will also see sharpened gut hooks on sheath and

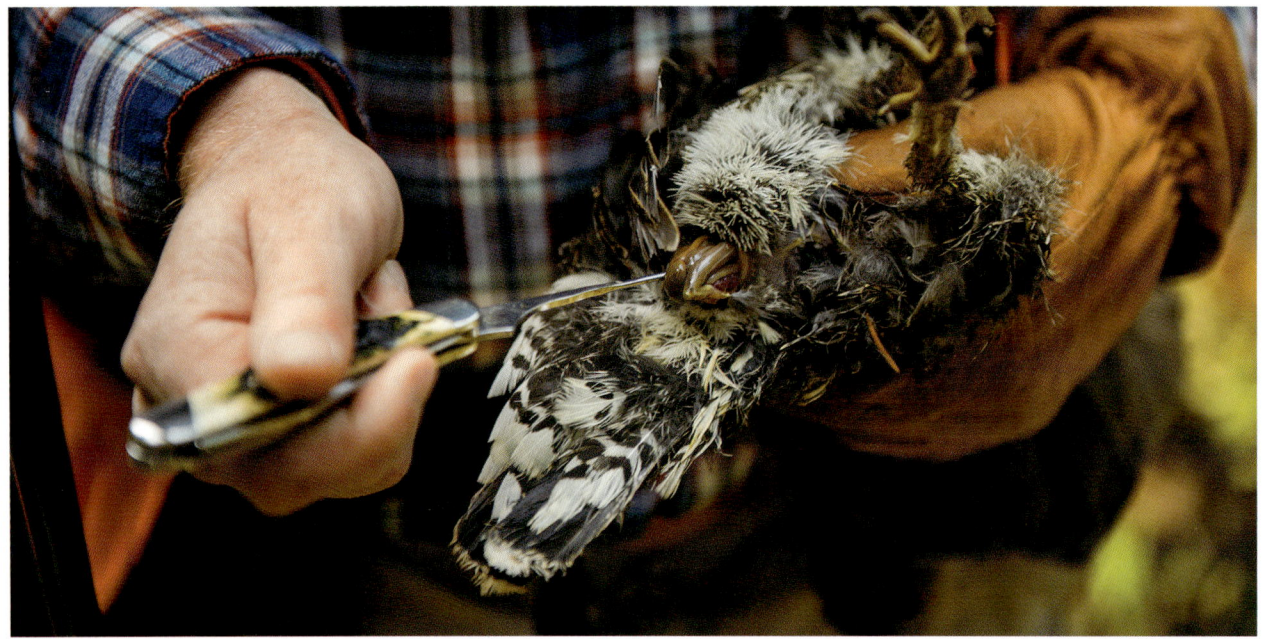

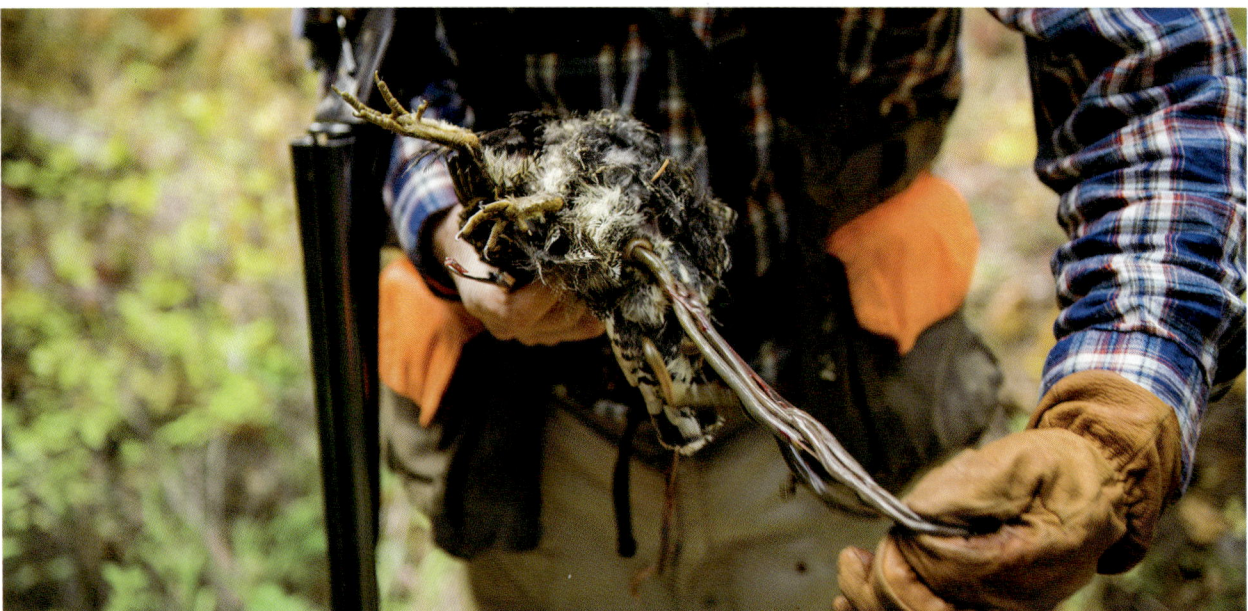

folding knives intended for use on big game. A gut hook with any sort of cutting edge is not for use on birds but furred game, whereas a gut hook with a blunted tip is intended for internal use. Very few bird hunters know how to put this tool to its intended function.

A bird gut hook is slim and generally about four inches long, with a bend in the terminal end that creates a "J" shape out of the entire tool. When a bird is shot, the hook can be inserted into the anal vent as deep as it will go, and then twisted a few times to entangle a loop of intestine. When carefully withdrawn from the anal vent, this loop of intestine can be pulled free of the cavity, and much of the connected viscera will come clear of the body along with it. Additional probing and removal will get the larger organs such as the gizzard and heart. Though this method does not result in a thoroughly clean bird, it neatly removes much of the heat-trapping entrails from the cavity, while leaving the bird itself both clean and by all appearances intact.

Plucking, Skinning, and Breasting

Removing the innards promptly allows the body to cool as quickly as possible, resulting in the mildest flavor. The reality, however, is that most upland hunters simply leave birds in the game bag until the day's end, then clean the lot. When dealing with an entire bird top to bottom, it is best to deal first with feathers or skin, and then to proceed to the body cavity as a secondary step. In this way body fluids and blood are contained until the feathers are removed. Regardless of methodology, I typically remove legs at the knee joint, head at the neck, and wings just adjacent to the body as an initial step. I do so by snipping all extremities off with a pair of garden-variety anvil hand pruners, available at any hardware store. If a more tidy carcass is warranted, the knee joint and elbow wing joint can be extended fully and then hyperextended while the tendons of the joint are cut (encircle the joint down to the bone with a knife and the tendons will sever). With the tendons cut, the bones will pull apart easily, and the remaining connective elements can be sliced through and the extremity released.

Upland birds are typically breasted, skinned whole, or plucked. Plucking is perhaps the most desirable method of prepping a bird, as it leaves a layer of flavorful subcutaneous fat on what is otherwise a very lean piece of meat. Plucking is, however, the most labor-intensive method of preparation. If plucking a bird, I would recommend doing so as quickly as possible after the bird is killed. While the flesh is still warm, you can dry pluck most upland birds fairly easily, without the skin tearing. To dry pluck, simply grasp a pinch of feathers between your fingers and thumb and pull away. The feathers of the breast, back, and legs will likely come off fairly easily. The longer feathers of the wings and tail will require a bit more work, but will be removed in kind. Scalding a bird in a hot water bath can and will facilitate the removal of feathers, but it's a bit of an art. You don't want to poach the flesh or overcook the skin. Look to scald the bird in 30-second immersions in a bath of 140- to

150-degree water. When tail or wing feathers pull out easily, the scalding process is complete. These thirty-second intervals will ensure a slow approach to the desired plucking stage.

If skinning a bird, the process is much simpler. Expose the skin covering the breastbone enough to allow a firm grasp of the breast skin, and simply tear it away from the bone. It will pull apart, and peel from the exposed muscle easily. In this manner, simply peel the bird as if it were a piece of fruit, exposing clean flesh and a remarkably tidy little package.

If breasting a bird, I recommend that the skin be peeled away from the breast entirely, then the meat can be filleted off the breastbone, or the breast can be removed bone-in. To remove the breast with the bone intact, slice the membrane that connects the breast to the body cavity. This will appear as a soft piece of thin tissue covering the abdominal region between the vent and the breast. Once cut, lift the breastbone up and back toward the bird's head, effectively prying it loose of the body cavity. Whatever connective elements remain will be at the shoulder joints, and these bones and tendons can be cut with the pruners. You will be left with a chunky piece of meat, ready for cooking in whole or filleting.

If the bird is skinned or plucked, and intended to serve whole, you will next need to remove the viscera from the body cavity. To do so, slice the aforementioned membrane to expose the cavity between the breast and the vent, being careful not to puncture the intestine. On either side of the anal vent you will feel a bony protrusion. These protrusions are the horns of the pelvis. When gutting a bird, I typically slice into the body cavity as stated and then reach into the cavity with two fingers and rake out what innards I can, pulling the mass down toward the anal vent and clear of the body. The intestines will remain connected to the vent, and they should not be torn free, as feces can taint the meat. With the mass of innards free of the cavity, I excise the vent by using the horns of the pelvis as a reference, and effectively circumscribing the vent with a sharp knife. This will release the mass of innards, and leave you with a largely clean bird.

Looking higher into the cavity, the lungs and heart will likely remain intact. The heart can be pulled free easily, but the lungs pose a bit more of a challenge. They are light pink, spongy masses nestled against and between the ribs on the bird's back, opposite the breast. Birds are highly susceptible to lung infection and disease, and if any nasty germs are lingering in a bird's system, it is likely that the lungs are involved. It is a good idea therefore to ensure that all lung tissue is removed before consuming. To get the lungs out, run the tip of a finger between the ribs and under the mass of lung tissue, freeing each lung from its connection. If you are able to remove the lungs in total, they will appear as two lobes of pink matter into which the indentation of the ribs is clearly visible. If they are torn during removal, the remaining pink tissue in the cavity will be easy to spot, and similarly easy to remove.

Whether a bird is skinned or plucked, it is critical to deal with the neck end of the breast as well. Presuming the head is removed before plucking or skinning, there will likely be a stump of neck remaining. This can be cut closer to the body for cosmetic reasons if so desired. Between the neck/spinal column and the breast there may remain a thin membrane or sack. This is the bird's crop. In gallinaceous birds, and in many but not all avian species, the crop is in essence a storage sack where food is held immediately upon ingestion. When a bird is killed, the crop may still be full of food, and therefore highly noticeable as a bulging, semi-transparent sack of grains, leaves, or insects. I like to examine the contents of the crop to see what the birds have been eating, as it can tell me a good deal about what sort of habitat I might find more of the same species lingering in.

Once the crop is examined, it can be pulled free, and will separate like a balloon from the

surrounding tissue. From there, the esophagus and trachea will be a pair of tubes traveling between the neck and breast down into the body cavity. These structures should be removed, though they are sometimes a challenge to get a purchase on. They can be pulled out from above, or pushed down through to the body cavity, but either way, the resulting carcass should be free of feathers on the outside and all organs on the inside. The carcass should then be rinsed thoroughly in cold water.

The final piece of knife work when prepping a bird deals with the oil pot, pope's nose, or more technically the pygostyle. This is the little pointed protrusion where the tail feathers collect. On the top of this appendage you will see a central node or gland that serves, in fowl, to allow not only for the manipulation of tail feathers, but also for the secretion of oils. This node should be excised. In many cases, I remove the pope's nose entirely, leaving a blunt end to my bird. Though somewhat coarse, this method ensures that oily secretions don't taint the meat.

When a bird is skinned or breasted, it is quite easy to see where shot has penetrated the body. Feathers will be pushed into the muscle tissue, and shot tracks will show as streaks of red that terminate in the muscle. Unless you fancy a trip to the dentist, as much shot as possible should be removed straightaway. This feat can be achieved by slicing into the muscle and teasing out shot and feathers with a knife tip, or with a spoon-like tool made from a flattened nail. Once as many pellets as possible have been removed, I like to brine my birds.

There are myriad tales of the sublime results of soaking a bird carcass in milk or buttermilk. Though altogether unnecessary, I have a habit of soaking my birds in a bath of cold salted water for up to 48 hours in the fridge, changing the brine if it becomes overly bloody. I'm no physicist, chemist, or voodoo priest, but I follow the ancient woods-wisdom that requires a sound brining process for a moist end product. Brining has the further benefit of removing trapped blood from the meat. If birds are to be cooked immediately

after brining, I proceed accordingly to the cooking stage. If they are to be frozen, I pat dry and vacuum seal the carcasses in an over-the-counter sealer, including a marinade in the bag if I am so inclined. With this last stage complete, and the aforementioned steps done in haste, I will achieve the mildest-tasting meat possible.

If the above processes sound intimidating, let me assure you that very little can go wrong in the cleaning and butchering process. In the end, provided there are no feathers left on the bird, all of what remains is edible if sufficiently cooked. If you look inside the body cavity and you see anything other than clean meat and bone, you have more cleaning to do. The best way to learn how to clean a bird is to just do it, and take your time. I can assure you it will be an educational experience.

Hanging and Aging

To many—the great Chef Hugh Fearnley-Whittingstall chief among them—the aforementioned haste in processing birds would be a travesty. When game is allowed to age a bit it develops a unique flavor that is prized by many, and it also becomes increasingly tender. It is true that in early days, and still in some circles, game birds were hung until high. In this case, birds hung by the neck were ostensibly deemed ready for the oven once sufficient decomposition had occurred to allow the head to separate from the body of its own accord. Though this failsafe method of ensuring sufficient aging may well simply be a bit of culinary hyperbole, well-aged birds are not for the faint of heart.

In slightly more reasonable terms, game birds do benefit from proper handling and aging. An

aged bird will tenderize noticeably, and the flavor will both mellow and deepen, which many find to be desirable. Aging should not, however, be undertaken with damaged or obviously gut-shot birds. If there is a notable smell of innards, or a significant amount of superficial blood or tearing, birds should be processed straightaway and rinsed well before cooking.

If a bird is shot cleanly, it can and likely should be cooled or aerated as quickly as possible, with the body left intact. Birds left to linger tight against your body in a game bag or vest are done no favors, so store them in a cool dry place with good air circulation as quickly as possible. Hanging birds by the neck is the traditional means of aging, as it allows any fluids to run out of the cavity and away. Birds should be hung in a room with an ambient air temperature of fifty to fifty-five degrees Fahrenheit.

The longer a bird hangs, the more tender it will become. In general terms, three to ten days is sufficient, assuming that deeper flavor develops increasingly with time. When the bird is deemed ready, it should be dry plucked instead of scalded, as the skin will have become more delicate. Once plucked, it can be eviscerated as usual. Though aged birds can be skinned, the skin and subcutaneous fat hold so much flavor that it often seems a shame to discard either.

Aged birds benefit from a rinse in cold water but should not require brining. They can then be prepared at once or frozen.

Incidentals

Many hunters always breast out their birds, either with the bone left in or in boneless fillets. There is no doubt that breasting is quick and easy, and that it leaves the hunter with the majority of the easily accessible meat on a game bird. To omit from the diet the thighs, legs, and wings, however, would be to forego an ample bit of meat. Preparation of these bits, and some others, requires some extra care.

Game birds are rarely stationary in the way that farm-raised or battery-raised chickens or turkeys are. Since they all rely on a run or fly response for their safety, game birds develop muscular but lean legs and wings, neither of which provide an abundance of meat. Legs especially are filled with tendons that, once cooked, can be a chore to eat around. In dealing with tendons, there are a few little backwoods tricks that might well be of use. To remove leg tendons on a hard-running bird like a pheasant, simply make a shallow cut around the skin of the leg just below the knee (this step is to be accomplished before the rest of the bird has been cleaned). Taking the leg in your hands, snap the lower leg bone clean through in the vicinity of the cut, creating a lower leg that is held together only by skin and connective tissue. Once the leg is broken, place the bird breast up on the ground and stand with a foot on each spread wing, essentially pinning the bird on its back. Grasp the foot of the broken leg and pull straight up, removing the lower leg by force from the rest of the pinned carcass. You will likely find that many of the leg tendons pull free with the lower leg and foot.

Another option for dealing with the sinewy bits of wild birds is to dust off your Crock-Pot, slow cooker, or pressure cooker. When pheasant legs and thighs are braised in stock, wine, tomatoes, or even water, the meat becomes tender and moist, and falls from the bone. Tendons and bones are picked from the cooked meat, which can then be shredded for use in a ragout, or tacos, or served in a barbeque-style sauce.

Taxidermy

The birds that we pursue as upland hunters are beautiful and rare. They are, in essence, nature's masterpieces, living works of art. In taxidermy, there is an opportunity to preserve them as such, and to remember those special moments in which we encountered them. Taxidermy, when done well, can suspend a memory in time.

Bird taxidermy is a difficult and time-consuming craft, and one that takes years to master. There are taxidermists of varying skill working throughout the country. A cursory web search or inquiry at your local gun shop will likely turn up several results, but take care; not all taxidermists are created equal. Look for someone who specializes in

birds, and ask to see a portfolio of work, or get some references. I have personally become the owner of some stunning bird mounts, and some stunningly awful ones. An ounce of prevention is worth a ton of cure where taxidermy is concerned, and I'd very much encourage you to shop around, and to send birds to the taxidermist that best fits your aesthetic and quality standard. Don't expect good taxidermy to come cheap or fast; be prepared to part with some bills, and to wait a few years at times to see your bird again. When you do, however, it will remain a vivid reminder of something quite special.

Taxidermists are fairly particular about the treatment and handling of birds that are meant to be mounted. Each has his or her own guidelines, but remember that though taxidermists are artists, they are not miracle workers. A badly torn-up, blood-soaked, and broken-beaked pheasant will likely never look as it did when alive, regardless of your desire or the taxidermist's skill. That said, a clean, unruffled bird can also be a real challenge for a taxidermist if handled improperly.

Birds intended for taxidermy are generally frozen and then shipped. The primary source of

concern when freezing a bird intact is dehydration and freezer burn. If a bird gets overly dry in the freezer, or if the skin gets freezer burned, the bird will not skin easily for the taxidermist, or retain feathers well. To ensure that a bird will be suitable for mounting, first keep it clean and protected after it is shot. Many old-timers suggest that the bird be placed in a nylon stocking to keep feathers from breaking, and provided you are careful, this can be a fine way to preserve the bird's quality over the course of the hunting day. Once home, however, carefully cut away the stocking and deal with the bird delicately.

A bird intended for mounting can be dealt with in one of two ways. The most common is to freeze the bird whole and dry. To do so properly, first wrap the head and feet in wet paper towels, and then tuck the head safely under the wing for protection. Smooth all feathers in their natural direction and place the bird in a ziplock bag. Remove whatever air you can from the bag, and place the resulting package in the freezer, ideally in a box of some sort. Birds become brittle when frozen, and dainty extremities such as toes and wing tips can break easily. Avoid placing birds in a frost-free freezer, as these units greatly expedite the dehydration process, and will freezer burn your bird.

A secondary tactic for bird storage is to freeze the entire bird in a ziplock bag full of water. Though this method sounds odd, it ensures that the bird will neither freezer burn nor break, and it can be stored nearly indefinitely. The whole shooting match can be sent to the taxidermist in a disposable cooler, but be prepared for a steep shipping charge due to weight.

Once you have prepared your bird for taxidermy, and you have selected the taxidermist that will do the work, follow his or her instructions on how best to ship your bird. As mentioned earlier, taxidermists each have their preferred method for preservation and shipping, and they will likely not be shy in telling you how best to proceed.

A Conservation Conversation

In *A Sand County Almanac*, Aldo Leopold wrote, "We abuse land because we regard it as a commodity belonging to us. When we see land as a community to which we belong, we may begin to use it with love and respect." This quotation alludes knowingly to what I find essential about being a hunter. Central to the process of becoming a hunter, and central to the identity you find upon arrival, is the community that Leopold speaks of. This is not just a community of peers, but rather a community of all things in nature. When you become a hunter, you cease to walk over the land; as a hunter, you become an element of that land, a cog in a remarkable living machine that is as old as the earth itself, and as timeless. Leopold spent a career reflecting on this community, and the role of humans within it. He sat and watched "like a mountain," as he put it, and he learned by reflective observation. He also took up a gun each autumn and went hunting, and learned a bit more about himself, and his human ecology, than he'd known before.

Leopold went on to say, "In short, a land ethic changes the role of *Homo sapiens* from conqueror of the land-community to plain member and citizen of it. It implies respect for his fellow-members, and also respect for the community as such." This construct is somewhat hard to grasp for most folks, simply because humans have the capacity, the resources, the vision, and the ingenuity to assert dominance over a natural system at will. We do so each and every day, as we increasingly live outside of nature. It is why we have survived and flourished, and it is also why, you might say, we have become disenchanted with, and certainly disconnected from, our natural world. We have lost our place in the community that allowed us a sense of place since time immemorial, and we've in turn become confused with our role.

It is ironic, therefore, that taking up a gun in fall and shooting a bird or two might serve to reestablish a fundamental philosophical and ecological order. It is ironic that in deploying a man-made machine and asserting dominance over a wild creature, or even more paradoxically a pen-raised creature, could help us regain a sense of ourselves. It is most ironic, I might add, that in light of the availability of prepackaged, precooked, profoundly inexpensive food we would ever choose to spend our time and money shooting at a piece of meat that, more often than not, sails away unscathed on downy wings. But we do this, and we love it, and we seek to do it again. In turn, it makes us care a little more about the birds we seek, and the places in which we seek them.

I am neither a student of psychology nor a student of philosophy, so I can't authoritatively say why we are drawn to hunting, or what it means that we are compelled in this way. I assume that we as humans were hunters for so long that it became a part of our wiring, and only fairly recently did we disconnect from a personal relationship with food acquisition. I can say, and with some confidence, that in becoming hunters, we are afforded an awareness of a new community, or perhaps better stated, a forgotten community, and one that our ancestors knew well. My friend Kurt Rinehart, who is one of the finest naturalists I know, often says that in being a hunter, he is offered a seat at the table. I love this analogy, in that it is resonant on a level that both speaks to basic human need and to essential human consciousness. In becoming a hunter, in North America anyway, that table is laid with a host of wild foods so delicate and rare that they are, in themselves, great treasures. They are offered to you in quantity for the cost of a hunting license and some wonderful days spent afield. Beside you at the table are people who, like you, see some

value in being outdoors, in taking responsibility for a linear connection to the food they eat, and the realities of it. There is a shared identity at the table, and a shared pride of place. There is, at root, community. But a seat at the table offers far more lasting value than simply a fine piece of meat, served in good company.

When you become a hunter, you attain a vested interest. Your very identity becomes reliant upon the nourishment of a species, the preservation of access, the maintenance of legislation that allows you to pick up a gun and go looking for a bird to shoot. In becoming a hunter, even a preserve hunter, you learn to be a part of a bigger construct, one in which animals rise from habitat, and you, also a piece of the habitat, aim to harvest them. In this construct, you match your skills against a bit of nature, and you witness unpredictability. You begin to notice things you rarely noticed before: the crackle of turning leaves on an October afternoon, the smell of prairie wheat, the glint of a cottonwood grove. These become things synonymous with your identity, and you begin to care for and about them. When that new office building threatens your pet woodcock covert, you take new notice. When an unknown blight does in your precious quail, you throw some money toward land stewardship and avian research. You become a part of a community that hinges on your involvement and investment. Without your care that community would suffer an incremental blow.

In short, hunting connects you, in a visceral way, to something of value. That something is a myriad of resources, natural and otherwise, that you suddenly see as a part of your personal geography. As a hunter, you begin to rely on those resources to provide you with a sense of place, a sense of self, and a sense of belonging. Within said community you are a member alongside the game, and the cover, and the greater ecosystem. You truly become

a citizen of what Leopold called a "land-community." As a citizen you are a stakeholder, one with both rights and obligations.

On a nuts-and-bolts level, hunters conserve the land community with dollars. At the time of this writing, nearly $200 million in hunters' federal excise taxes are allocated annually to fund agencies that support wildlife-management programs, the purchase of land that remains accessible to hunters, and the development and delivery of hunter's education and safety classes. Hunting organizations spend time and money to maintain a voice of advocacy for wildlife and for habitat, on both a state and federal level. License fees and hunter's excise taxes on guns, ammunition, and various other sporting necessities are channeled directly into conservation efforts on a local and national scale. There is little doubt that hunters are among the greatest champions of game and habitat, and on more than just a fiduciary stage.

I firmly believe that in hunting, we cannot help but learn to become better stewards of the land and the critters that exist upon it. As hunters, we are reminded that we are but one species of those critters, albeit with a bit more firepower and impact than most others. As hunters we are out with our boots on the ground, gaining intimacy with the land community in a way we otherwise could not. We become, as poet Marge Piercy once described, "natives of that place." We revisit this land community with a hunter's eyes, and an acute awareness that the experience we seek hinges on the health of that community. We pull our seat up to the table and we care deeply about who is in attendance, and what is being served. In the absence of this intimacy, conservation becomes something remote and academic. In the presence of this intimacy, with blood beneath our fingernails and mud on our pant cuffs, it becomes something worth fighting for.

Sundries

Chapter 10

Sundries

As in so many of life's adventures, the journey through the uplands can lead down myriad pathways, and into myriad corners of the sport. The road you follow will be directed by your personal aesthetic, the species you prefer to hunt, and the opportunities that fall nearest at hand. You may become a dedicated pheasant shooter who makes an annual pilgrimage to the corn stubble and shelter belts of the Dakotas to chase ditch parrots under a massive sky. You may find yourself a quail devotee, with a penchant for twenty-eight-gauge double guns and twelve-year-old bourbon. You may, like me, choose a life of misery, wherein ruffed grouse fill your dreams and, in daylight, thunder out from places unknown, rarely presenting a makeable shot.

Regardless of the path you follow, or the subculture of upland hunting that you find yourself in, it is a benefit from the start to know that in the uplands, diversity abounds. There are specific hunting styles and opportunities that you may encounter, several of which I will describe in detail here, as they present a unique set of circumstances for you, the hunter, to research and explore.

Doves

Doves are among the most prevalent of North America's upland game birds, though in truth their denomination as such is somewhat of a question. Doves are not chicken-like, gallinaceous birds, but

rather songbirds. Nonetheless they are prized on the plate by many American wingshooters. They also provide some of the most challenging shooting of all hunted bird species due to their swift and erratic flight. They are hunted in the early season, typically in September, and the traditional dove opener of September 1 makes for the busiest single day of wingshooting nationwide, and possibly in all the world. Needless to say, doves are not an incidental species.

Doves are traditionally pass-shot when coming from the roost to feed in grain fields, going from feeding grounds to grit or water, or returning from the grain fields to roost for the night. Pass-shooting simply means that rather than rising up before an advancing hunter, or settling into a decoy spread as in waterfowling, doves are mainly shot while flying from point A to point B between the aforementioned destinations. For this reason, doves are often taken while traveling at full speed, typically at moderate height, and often without displaying any immediate inclination to slow down. Shots are primarily straight crossers or high overhead shots, depending on the shooter's aspect with regard to the flight path. Doves are small targets, and phenomenally challenging to hit on the wing.

Of the dove species hunted in North America, the usual suspects include the mourning dove (far and away the most widely distributed), the white-winged dove, and the non-endemic Eurasian collared dove (which has no closed season). Dove limits are comparatively large, with a fifteen-bird bag the standard as of this writing. Though not hunted throughout North America, most states have an extant dove season, particularly those states rich in agriculture.

A dove hunt is most often a convivial affair, with painstaking observance to tradition in some regions. By and large, a group of shooters will gather around a grain field or watering area during the active periods for birds (i.e., midmorning or late afternoon). Lightly concealed and dressed for seasonable heat, shooters make haste to shoot doves as they fly through shooting zones that overlay the field, and shooters often bear witness to, and comment on, the successes and requisite failures of their fellow shooters. Birds are picked up either by hand or by retrieving dogs, and on a good shoot, the action can be steady. Beware that other species such as American kestrels can be mistaken for doves in flight; as kestrels are a federally protected species, the "oops" defense won't take you far.

Once an organized dove shoot is complete, there ensues some degree of planned revelry. Typically, libations are offered, and a grill is put to use, firing dove breasts wrapped in bacon. A jalapeno pepper nestled into the mix is a regional adaptation in much of Texas and the South. This whole affair makes for some fine eating; dove breasts are dark and rich in flavor, little more than a bite-sized morsel but delicious when served quickly in the field. An offer of participation in a traditional Southern dove hunt is not to be passed up.

If hunting doves on one's own, particularly in a new area, remember certain details. First, doves need water, and they will gravitate to it at some point during the day. Scout water holes and tanks, and take note of which direction the birds fly in from, and where they depart to. This will inform your concealed placement, and make for better shooting, dependent somewhat on wind direction. Doves respond well to motion decoys. Spinning-wing dove decoys on posts, similar to those made by the MOJO Company, will dramatically increase your success. So too will the use of a good retriever. Doves often fall in thick cover, and their coloration can make them challenging to find on the ground. Mark birds rigorously and pick them up quickly, or several will be lost. If hunting in hot climes in the early season, clean and cool your birds quickly.

If hunting around an agricultural field with friends, be extraordinarily cautious of low shots. Always ensure that a dove in flight is framed against blue sky before a shot is taken.

Requisite equipment for dove shooting can vary, but many folks feel that a cartridge belt or pouch is necessary, as is a tule seat or field stool. Recall that orange is not to be worn, and that drab colors or light camo patterns are considered appropriate. Guns down to twenty-eight gauge are appropriate, and longer shots may necessitate fairly tight chokes.

Though I hate to relegate the shooting of live creatures as anything to be taken lightly, I will say that dove shooting is phenomenal for your wing-shooting skills. The opportunity to shoot frequently at nimble birds, and to be required to establish a smooth-swinging motion, will be invaluable down the road. I would highly recommend that a developing shooter seek out the opportunity to shoot doves, if for no better reason than it is a great way to hone shooting skills, with the benefit of some fine kitchen provender at the day's end.

Driven Bird Shooting

If you recall from chapter two, our North American bird-hunting tradition evolved largely in response to a European tradition, with established roots in the United Kingdom. The British Isles continue to be the cultural heartland of all driven

bird shooting, both for wild red grouse on the moors and for reared pheasants and partridges on private estates. The driven bird tradition is well established overseas, and has gained some ground in recent years as a sought-after experience for traveling American shooters, with a model that has been replicated stateside.

Driven bird shooting is just that. Birds are pushed physically by an advancing line of beaters and their leashed dogs, often toward a tree line or other physical impediment that impels the birds into flight. Beyond this physical obstacle is a line of shooters, distributed on stations known as pegs. As the birds clear the impediment, they fly high over the line of guns, and the birds that traverse the piece of sky above a given peg are shot, or, more often, shot at. After a drive is complete, and sometimes during, the birds are picked up by a team of aptly named pickers-up and their dogs. After the line of beaters reaches the physical impediment mentioned above, the drive is signaled as over, often by means of a horn blast. The pegs may then be shifted, or the line may be relocated, before a new drive takes place. This process is quite ritualized in the United Kingdom, with a strict code of ethics and customs.

The beauty of a driven shoot is the unique presentation of the shots. With pheasants and partridges, driven shoots are judged for quality based on the height of the presented birds. The finest shoots claim to have birds that fly over the line of guns at up to sixty yards of elevation, making for dearly challenging shots for all but the best. Particularly difficult is the fact that these oncoming shots are taken while leaning back, and swinging the gun through the bird to the point that the barrels cover it, and said bird disappears from sight.

Perhaps the most highly esteemed sort of driven shooting is the extraordinarily exclusive Scottish grouse drive, wherein birds come in fast and low over the heathered moors, passing stone buttes or stations. It is a shot rarely seen in any other sort of game shooting, and it makes for some fast and furious action.

Due to management practices, costs, and various other contingencies, a true driven shoot is inordinately expensive. If you calculate the costs associated with rearing birds on the ground in a natural environment, maintaining a piece of ground conducive to a drive, then hiring a staff of beaters, loaders, and pickers-up to execute the driven day, the numbers will be staggering. Hence, a true driven shoot is quite rare in the United States, and even on the traditional estates of the United Kingdom it can be prohibitively expensive. Grouse shooting on the moors of Scotland is even further out of reach. There are a select few true driven opportunities in North America, and they are not inexpensive to take part in.

American shooters have developed a modified version of the driven shoot that does a decent job of replicating the presentations of birds without the challenging logistics. This event is variously known as the tower or continental shoot, and it essentially requires birds to be thrown from an elevated tower or topographic feature over a line of shooters. Typically, after a given number of birds have been presented, the pegs are shifted and the shoot resumes. The shoot ends when the preordained number of birds has been presented—for example a 400-bird shoot.

When done well, continental shoots present high-flying birds in a naturalized setting, where presentations are similar to driven birds, and high birds are paramount. Generally, continental shoots offer high-volume shooting without the requisite costs of land and infrastructure, though the cost of the birds themselves can be high due to volume. These shoots are wildly popular at gun clubs throughout the United States, with the Orvis Sandanona Shooting Grounds in Millbrook, New York, hosting a series of favorites.

Of note in driven or continental shoots is that significant etiquette and safety rules apply. If invited to a driven shoot, assume it will be a formal affair, with appropriate dress required. Ask your host whether tweeds are part of the dress code, as they may well be. On a UK or European driven shoot, tweeds are de rigueur, and the costume is as much a part of the experience as the actual shooting.

As the shooting in a driven-style shoot can be fast and furious, you may occasionally see identical pairs of guns used by a single shooter, and handed to a loader after the guns are empty. Two identical guns are called a matched pair, and they are typically built to order for a dedicated driven bird shooter. The premise here is that one gun can be emptied, handed to the loader, and reloaded while a fresh gun, identical in every way to the first, is handed to the shooter. This rapid orchestration of loader and shooter is a lovely dance, especially when the rhythms synchronize. Matched pairs are not required, but be aware that they may be present.

Because high pheasants in particular require some impact for ethical shooting, tight chokes make some sense where driven birds are concerned. Twelve-, sixteen-, and twenty-gauge guns, choked modified or tighter, are standard. Long barrels allow for the smooth swing necessary for adequate performance. Twenty-eight-gauge guns on a driven or continental shoot are likely to be viewed as distasteful and somewhat unethical. Semi-automatics are almost never seen.

Due to the volume of shells required over the course of a driven day, it is likely that you will want a cartridge bag or speed bag. Speed bags are used by shooters, or loaders for that matter, to hold upward of 100 loose shells. The bag is worn over the shoulder like a purse, and the gun is loaded out of it. Speed bags are generally leather or heavy canvas.

From an etiquette standpoint, it is valuable to remember that pegs are assigned early in the day at random, often through an orchestrated draw. Though each peg will likely receive an adequate number of shots, they will also be rotated throughout the day. Your "air space" will be fairly

obvious with respect to that of other shooters. Never *ever* shoot low birds or birds immediately exiting the tower. These shots put throwers or beaters in harm's immediate way, and may be cause for dismissal from a shoot, or at best a small likelihood of a return invitation. If you frequently poach the birds of a neighboring peg, that too is a sign of poor form. Finally, if you "mop up" frequent cripples on behalf of a neighbor, you may be seen as a bit of a braggart, which never bodes well for the social health of the day.

Driven and continental shoots are a glorious opportunity for high-volume shooting at unique presentations. They are further compelling if you have mobility issues or prefer to not follow a big-running dog through the field. Granted, driven and continental shoots are truly shoots, with the "hunting" aspect shifting into somewhat murky territory, at least semantically. The shooting will be solid, though, and the experience memorable. There are those dedicated few who choose to shoot only driven birds.

Sporting Clays

In my experience, there is nothing worse than waiting all year for that glorious season opener, only to miss the few shots that arise. It is remarkable how quickly shooting skills can rust in the off-season, and poor shooting can turn what should be a fine day into a study in vexation. A bit of practice in the off-season can make a world of difference in hunting success, while also being an enjoyable exercise in its own right.

Clays games are likely the most obvious avenue for off-season practice at game shooting. That said, certain games make more sense than others. Trap and skeet are timeless classics, but they both present

replicable shots that can be mastered analytically and scientifically. Once a given shot at skeet or trap is broken down, training and practice at that one shot can lead to mastery. Now let me be clear that any and all shooting practice will make a shooter better, provided the gun fits and the shooter's form and mechanics are sound. It is my firm belief, however, that the game of sporting clays replicates a much more natural field-shooting experience.

A sporting clays course is composed of a series of stations, all of which offer diverse shots that make optimal use of the topography and landscape. I recommend that when shooting sporting clays, shooters begin in a low-gun position, meaning that the gun is not premounted on the shoulder. In a hunting environment, hunters do not walk with the gun premounted, and practice should be made to mimic real-world hunting scenarios. Instinctive, intuitive shooting skills, and confidence in those skills, are built with time and practice. Sporting clays offer the best opportunity for this practice.

If you wish to participate in sporting clays, opportunities abound. With rapidly growing interest in the game, clays courses are popping up throughout North America. As in all things, facilities can vary in quality, cost, and scope, but I would venture a guess that a public clays facility exists inside of a two-hour drive from your location. Orvis Sandanona is among the country's finest sporting clays courses. It is a beautiful facility in a wooded, pastoral setting only one-and-a-half hours from Manhattan.

 # Afterword

Tomorrow is September 1. On that day, upland season opens in Montana, and despite summerlike temperatures and a high prairie sun, the autumn will begin again. It's hot back home in Vermont, too, but "the season," as I've grown accustomed to calling it, is still long weeks away. Montana cannot boast the earliest upland season in North America; that distinction goes to Alaska and her native ptarmigan, which have, in seasons past, tempted me too. But regardless of the calendar, the smell of Hoppe's powder solvent and the sight of bird dogs in fighting trim announces the season with conviction, and I find it where I can. Tomorrow birds will rise before dogs and guns, and some will become flesh and feather in my hands. Those that fall, and those that sail away, will remain footnotes in an almanac of birds found and birds put to flight, feathers and flushes and food to sustain me, and wing-beats to match the fluttering of my humble heart.

I will get up early tomorrow, in the cool of the day, and drink coffee in the dark. The shells will be dumped into the shell pouch of my vest, and I'll carry far more of them than a limit of sharptails and Hungarian partridges could possibly command. I'll dress warm in the cool of the dawn, but prepare to shed layers as the sun gains perspective and takes an angle across the prairie grass. I'll carry ample water for the dogs, but it won't be quite enough, and I'll circle back to the truck at intervals for more. I'll swap out tired dogs, running the younger ones in the lee of the brag dogs, who I've been waiting to watch all year. The dogs will be as eager as I am, and they'll overdo it in their zeal; the day will be done before high afternoon. It's early season after all, and in our legs we'll feel the distance between the present day and last year's closing one, a long nine months before.

I hope to find sharptail grouse in the broken grasses between the buttes. Big-running dogs will struggle in the heat, battling their own requirements for oxygen against those breaths dedicated to bird scent. The birds will be coveyed up still, and the popcorn flushes will come ahead of the first tentative points; birds bouncing up and out in ones and twos. I'll try to leave the young of the year, noting in flight the small size, and the tentative plans for evasion. That said, I'll be eager too, and

I'll likely shoot a few of the young birds just out of excitement. These I will hold in my hands with that mixture of joy and regret, feeling the presence of animation suspended, vibrancy gone limp. I'll wish for a second I could put them back. Then I'll poke them in my game bag and move on.

On the grassy hillsides the Huns will rise in unison, great big coveys erupting together from waves of knee-high grass. They will confound me no doubt, flying en masse and rising close, but never quite presenting the easy shots that my rusty habits require. Flock shots will find all of the negative space, and lead pellets will poke holes in nothing at all except the tableau of buttes and rangy flatlands. Invariably I'll relearn old lessons, and wind up with a few of the gray-russet birds too, smaller than their sharp-tailed cousins but no less precious.

At midday the sun will be high and the dogs will be hot, and it may be time for a break. There will be some birds on ice, field dressed but feathered, awaiting a mellowing of days back in the barn. I'll stop for lunch at a small-town diner, and I'll drink iced tea, and share with my companions the stories that we were there to see transpire in real time. No doubt the retelling will be sweeter than the tea, and the shots we made good on longer than the expanse of sky; our hearts will remain as light as dust motes floating through the light of the diner's storefront glass.

In the waning day I'll hunt again, in hopes of a limit, but happy with what I get. Birds will be grouped back up for the roost, and the shadows will be long. I'll run the dogs around the remains of a homesteader's cabin, and I may pick up a bird or two, just to add to the larder. I'll leave time for a momentary sit down, just as the sun breaches the westward sky, and I'll chew on dead grass stems and let the dogs roll, and I won't say anything at all.

As a bird hunter, I find meaning in something as ephemeral as changing seasons, and something as actual as blood beneath my fingernails. These realities punctuate my days and years, giving me an identity far bigger, and more full, than my game bag. It is not hard to become poetic as a bird hunter. It may be harder, in fact, to avoid the inevitable mellowing, and deepening, of the identity it provides. In hunting I find logic in a parade of days, and the dogs that steal space in my bed, and the evenings by the February fire where I just sit with a drink and a gun open in my lap, daydreaming out across the seasons. This is what provides me a lens through which to see the world, and see myself in it. This is what I love.

Tomorrow is September 1, and the start of this return to something, and the ongoing passage through it. Montana will be ours, but so will the Vermont popple whips, and the Dakota milo strips, and the Alaska willows. I will share this with my fellow hunters. There is a universality to what I gain from being an upland hunter; a joy that is hard to describe. It is not something that comes and goes with the seasons, but it is emphatic when the light changes, and the earth turns golden, and flushing birds fill my heart once more.

So with that I offer you upland hunting. It is yours for the taking, a gift to savor and to share. I warn you, though, that it will creep into your unattended moments: gun oil will stain your furniture, and bird dog puppies will steal your place on the pillow. These things too are wonderful. These are things of essential beauty, and I envy you the joy of discovering them.

# Glossary

action. The portion of the gun that merges the buttstock and the barrel(s). The receiver houses the functional moving parts that deploy the shotshell. These parts include the trigger, hammer, firing pin, et al. See also ***receiver***.

autoloader. An autoloading gun features a mechanism that ejects a spent shell and inserts an unfired round into the chamber with each pull of the trigger. The autoloader requires no manual loading with successive shots, and is the most mechanized of the shotgun actions. See also ***semi-automatic action***.

backing. A dog work term. When a pointing dog backs, it honors the point of another dog. Dog 1 finds scent and goes on point; dog 2, upon identifying this initial point, backs dog 1, freezing so as not to run over or bump any birds on the ground. Dog 1 points birds; dog 2 backs by pointing dog 1.

barrel. A tubular structure that contains and directs the explosion that results from the detonation of a cartridge. Said containment results in projectiles (shot) being propelled from a shotgun in the direction of a target.

barrel wall. The physical structure that makes up the tubular barrel. Measured in thickness or wall thickness.

bead. A spherical bead on the muzzle end of the rib or barrel that ostensibly helps align the shooter's sight with the target. Occasionally there is a center bead as well, located at some distance between the muzzle and the breech.

beater. An individual whose role on a driven shoot is to physically push birds toward a line of guns. Beaters often walk with dogs and make a considerable commotion in order to impel birds into flight in the desired direction.

beavertail fore-end. A fore-end on a side-by-side shotgun that extends beyond the width of, and partially wraps around, the barrels. The beavertail allows greater purchase on the fore-end, and protects the forward hand from hot barrels. See also ***splinter fore-end***.

bird. An exclamation that indicates a bird has flushed, and it is to be watched. Used to alert fellow hunters that a bird is up, and to keep watch.

bird necker. A tool used to dispatch a bird. The necker is a plier-like device that separates the vertebrae of the neck without breaking the skin.

black powder. The precursor of modern ***smokeless powder***. Black powder is simply a chemical propellant that, when burned, creates an explosive expansion of gasses used to move a projectile. Unlike smokeless powder, black powder leaves largely solid by-products of combustion.

blaze orange. Also known as ***safety orange*** or ***hunter orange***, blaze is a shade of orange used

in hunting clothing to alert other hunters to an individual's presence.

bluing. A chemical process applied to steel that partially protects the metal from rust. Blued steel has a deep, blue-black luster. Barrels, trigger guards, and various other shotgun components are regularly blued.

bogsucker. A colloquial name for the American woodcock.

bolt. A mechanical element of either a pump or semi-automatic shotgun that blocks the rear of the chamber and houses the firing pin (i.e., serves as the breechblock). The bolt also assists in removing (ejecting) the spent shell and replacing it with a new shell retrieved from the magazine.

bore. The interior surface of the barrel. Where *barrel wall* describes the three-dimensional structure that comprises the barrel, the bore is simply the two-dimensional surface.

brass. The metal base of a standard shotshell. High-brass shells often contain a heavier powder charge than low-brass shells, but this trend is a holdover from the days of black powder and paper hulls. See also *high-brass shell* and *low-brass shell*.

break action. A breech-loading firearm action in which the action and barrels are hinged with a hinge pin. In a break-action gun, barrels rotate perpendicular to the bore axis to expose chambers for loading and unloading. It is widely considered the safest action type, as when open it is visually and physically incapable of discharge.

breech. The barrel end nearest the shooter, and the end into which the shell is loaded.

breech-loader. A gun that is loaded from the breech end, as opposed to a muzzle-loader.

buckshot. Large pellets used in a shotgun to kill big game, such as deer or varmints.

bump. A term used with pointing dogs. When a dog bumps a bird, it fails to point, but flushes the bird inadvertently. Also known as busting a bird.

butt. The flat surface of the buttstock that rests against the shoulder.

buttplate. Often made of hard rubber, plastic, horn, or hardwood, the buttplate caps the end-grain of the shotgun butt.

buttstock. The opposite of the forestock or fore-end, the buttstock is the component of the stock behind the action, which rests against the shoulder and cheek of the shooter.

caliber. The measurement of the inside diameter of the barrel, expressed in decimal components of an inch. A quarter-inch inside diameter would represent a .250 caliber, expressed as two-fifty caliber. It is rarely an exacting measure.

cartridge. The cartridge contains the primer, powder, wad, and shot. When deployed, the cartridge hurls projectiles from the barrel.

cartridge bag. This traditional purse-like accoutrement holds several boxes of shells, often during a driven shoot.

cast. Extent of offset left (cast on) or right (cast off) between the midline of the barrels and the center of the butt.

chamber. A recess at the breech end of the barrel in which the cartridge sits awaiting detonation. Chambers are measured in gauge and length, e.g., three-inch twelve gauge. Gauge and chamber length in modern guns is often stamped on the barrel. Older guns should be measured by a gunsmith.

choke. A constriction in the bore of a shotgun that occurs at the muzzle, designed to concentrate the dispersal of shot.

choke tube. Short steel cylinders that screw into threads in the muzzle of a shotgun barrel to achieve various degrees of choke.

cocking. To put the shotgun mainspring under tension in anticipation of firing.

comb. The top portion of the buttstock that receives the shooter's cheek.

continental shoot. Similar, but with subtle semantic differentiation from, a ***tower shoot***. The continental shoot revolves around high birds released from a tower that present high-volume shooting in the fashion of a driven shoot.

cover. The habitat in which any given species of upland bird is found.

covert. The habitat specifically in which grouse and woodcock are found. The term is somewhat specific to the northeastern and upper midwestern regions of North America.

covey. A group of upland birds. Birds such as quail, which tend to group up throughout the lifespan, are known as coveying birds.

covey rise. When a covey of birds is flushed, the initial flush often occurs en masse, presenting multiple shots. This flush of birds is called a covey rise.

cylinder choke. The choke designation that affords the least constriction, and therefore the widest pattern.

Damascus. A barrel material that institutes a twist of iron and steel formed around a mandrel and then forge welded. Typically considered for use with black-powder cartridges.

ditch parrot. A pseudonym for the common pheasant. Named for the pheasant's propensity to hide in low, congested wetland areas.

dog handler. The individual in command of the dogs on any given hunt.

drams equivalent (dr. eq.). A denomination of powder charge in a given shotshell.

drop. A degree of vertical offset of the buttstock below the top of the barrels (rib).

dry pluck. To pluck a bird without first scalding it in hot water. This is best done while the carcass is still warm with life.

early release. A practice of stocking in which birds are released before the season and allowed to naturalize to the environment, replicating the closest approximation of a wild population.

eject. To dynamically remove the spent shell from the chamber, often by means of a mechanical ejector.

firing pin. A thin cylinder housed in the bolt or the action that, when deployed, strikes the primer of the cartridge to initiate detonation.

fixed choke. The opposite of ***screw-in choke***, wherein choke is built integrally into the barrel.

flight conditioned. Pen-raised birds that have been afforded the opportunity to fly in captivity. Flight-conditioned birds will fly hard and fast when released into the hunting fields, and are therefore desirable.

flights (woodcock). An arrival of migrating woodcocks in number in a given covert. Individuals of the group are called flight birds.

flush. The act of an upland bird taking flight, typically from the ground.

flusher. A dog used to set birds into flight.

forcing cone. A portion of the barrel forward of the chamber that transitions the barrel diameter from the chamber (outside diameter of the shell) to bore (inside diameter of the shell).

fore-end. The portion of the gun stock held by the forward hand. The fore-end resides under

the barrel(s). Also known as the forearm or forestock.

full choke. The tightest common choke constriction, providing the tightest possible pattern.

gauge. A descriptor of the inside diameter of the barrel, or the diameter of the bore.

gorget. The black mask occurring on some game bird species, namely the chukar partridge and the closely related red-legged partridge.

grains. A unit of weight used to describe powder charge.

grip. A portion of the gunstock held by the shooter's rear hand.

guide model vest. A hunting vest made for professional use.

gun dog. A dog trained to locate, point, flush (i.e., make fly), and/or retrieve game.

gun fit. The degree to which a gun's stock dimensions suit an individual shooter. Guns can be built or modified to fit.

gun slip. A simple case for a shotgun, typically opened at one end and secured with a buckle.

gunfitter. One who, like a tailor, measures the optimal stock dimensions for a shooter, typically by means of a *try gun*.

gut hook. A blunted hook used to remove the bulk of organs through the anal vent of a bird, affording rapid cooling.

hammer. An element of a gun that is held under spring tension. When released, the hammer acts on the firing pin to detonate the shotshell.

heel. The top of the butt of a gun stock.

high-brass shell. A cartridge with a comparatively substantial brass base. Often correlates with a comparatively high powder charge.

hinge pin. The pin that allows a break-action gun to pivot into an open or a closed position.

HIP number. A migratory bird harvest information program number. This number provides a method by which state and federal wildlife agencies are developing more reliable estimates of the number of migratory birds harvested throughout the country.

honor. See *backing*.

hung until high. An Anglophile's term for birds aged until the meat is well ripened.

hunter orange. See *blaze orange*.

hunter's safety card. A certificate of completion of a hunter's safety course. Regularly required for the purchase of a hunting license.

hunter's safety course. A course of study mandated in most states as a prerequisite for buying a hunting license. The course covers all facets of safe gun handling and hunter etiquette.

hunting abstracts. In any given state, the list of rules and regulations for legal hunting. Abstracts are often published online as well as in print.

hup. A command used to sit a spaniel or other flushing dog in the field.

lay birds. When hunting coveying birds such as quail, the initial covey rise will disperse the majority of birds, though often a few remaining singles will hold tight and flush late. These are lay birds.

length of pull. The distance from the front trigger to the center of the butt.

low-brass shell. Comparatively short brass base for a cartridge, typically reserved for light loads.

low-gun position. A gun held off the shoulder. When shooting clays, a gun can either be held at the low-gun or *premounted* position. The low-gun position requires a gun mount.

magazine. A spring-operated reservoir for additional cartridges, found in a repeating firearm such as a semi-automatic or pump.

mark. See *bird*.

mil-spec. When used in reference to shooting glasses, the military-approved degree of shatter resistance.

mud bat. A pseudonym for the American woodcock.

muzzle. The end of the barrel out of which the explosion is channeled. The opposite of the breech.

muzzle-loader. A gun loaded from the muzzle end, typically with black powder. Considered an antiquated design in shotguns.

oil pot. A colloquialism for the pygostyle, or the fleshy protuberance at the base of a game bird's tail. This region contains a preening gland, and should be removed in the dressing process.

open pattern. A comparatively wide dispersal of shot.

over/under. A break-action shotgun in which the barrels are oriented one above the other, affording a single sighting plane.

pass-shooting. To shoot while birds are passing at height, rather than intending to settle into decoys or otherwise nearby.

pattern. The shape of the shot swarm expressed two dimensionally. In essence, the cluster of holes that would appear on a paper target shot by a shotgun.

peg. The station at which a shooter stands in a driven, tower, or continental shoot.

pickers-up. Those who, with dogs, retrieve shot game in a driven shoot.

point. To suspend the pounce instinct in a dog, affording a gunner an indication of where game lies.

point dead. Some dogs that will not retrieve will still point a dead bird. This action helps hunters retrieve dead birds on their own.

pointer. A dog genetically disposed to point game. Colloquially, the English pointer is often referred to as simply a pointer.

pope's nose. See *oil pot*.

powder. The explosive chemical compound found in a cartridge.

powder charge. The amount of powder encased in a shell.

premounted. A gun held on the shoulder in anticipation of the shot.

preserve. A shooting area in which game birds are introduced and managed. A hunting preserve requires licensure, and is afforded hunting laws independent of those set by the state.

primer. A small disc of highly explosive compound fitted into the head (bottom) of a cartridge. When struck by the firing pin, the primer detonates and ignites the powder charge, resulting in the shot.

proofing. The firing of a gun in a controlled environment with an extra-heavy load to ensure structural integrity and safety.

proof house. A controlled environment in which proofing takes place.

pump action. An action type wherein the fore-end is cycled back and then forward to eject a spent shell and reload a new one from the magazine.

pygostyle. See ***oil pot***.

receiver. The frame or action body of a shotgun that holds the mechanism for firing.

recoil pad. A pad affixed to the shotgun butt to lessen felt recoil.

repeating firearm. A firearm that can cycle multiple shots in succession, namely a semi-automatic or pump action.

rib. A metal strip affixed on top of or between the barrels to help with pointing.

safety orange. See ***blaze orange***.

screw-in choke. Tapered and threaded steel cylinders that thread into the shotgun muzzle(s) to allow shooters to change chokes in a barrel. The opposite of ***fixed choke***.

semi-automatic action. A style of repeating firearm action wherein each trigger pull fires the gun, ejects the spent cartridge, loads a fresh round from the magazine, and cocks the mainspring/hammer. See also ***autoloader***.

shell. See ***cartridge***.

shooting flying. A British term for wingshooting, or shooting birds in flight.

shot. Metal pellets propelled from a shotgun after detonation of the shotshell.

shot column. The three-dimensional swarm of shot as it travels through space.

shotshell. See ***cartridge***.

shot size. Size of the individual metal pellets fired from a shotgun. Denominations are in whole and half sizes, with the larger the number indicating the smaller the actual pellet (i.e., No. 9 shot is smaller than No. 4).

shot spread. Often used interchangeably with ***pattern***, describing the circumference and density of the pellets in two dimensions.

shot string. In essence, the length of the column occupied by shot in flight, after detonation of a cartridge.

shotgun. A firearm designed to propel a number of small metal pellets called shot. A shotgun is loaded with shotshells, which come in a variety of shapes and sizes.

side-by-side. A shotgun in which the barrels are situated side by side in a lateral plane.

skeet. An established game of clay targets with specific rules. Also, a denomination of choke, namely Skeet 1 and Skeet 2, which are slightly tighter than cylinder and improved cylinder respectively.

slide action. A common name for a pump action.

smokeless powder. An improvement upon ***black powder*** in modern cartridges, smokeless has a host of virtues that make it more efficient and user-friendly than black powder.

speed bag. See ***cartridge bag***.

splinter fore-end. A slim fore-end style classically used in a side-by-side gun. See also ***beavertail fore-end***.

sporting clays. A popular clays game that replicates real game presentations.

staunch. A descriptor of a dog that will not budge upon the point or flush even after the shot is fired. A staunch dog releases upon command.

steady. See ***staunch***.

stock. The nonmetal element of a gun that a shooter holds.

tight pattern. The close unity of pellets in a pattern resulting from ample choke.

timberdoodle. A colloquialism for the American woodcock.

toe. The bottom of the shotgun butt.

top rib. The rib that falls on top of the barrel.

tower shoot. A shoot in which birds are released from a tower, simulating the high overhead shots desirable in a driven shoot. See also **continental shoot**.

trail. An encompassing term for the innards of the American woodcock, typically sautéed and served in or on the bird.

trap. A formal clays game focused on going-away targets.

trigger. A slim lever on a gun that releases the mainspring and initiates detonation.

try gun. A working shotgun retrofitted to have adjustable stock dimensions. Once dimensions are deemed optimal for a shooter, they can be recorded and translated into a new or modified shotgun.

upland game birds. Edible species of birds that do not spend appreciable periods of time in or on the water (that is to say, they are not waterfowl). They are chiefly species of the order *Galliformes*, which is composed of heavy-bodied, chicken-like birds. The legal pursuit of these species is sanctioned, in North America anyway, by state, provincial, or federal law.

upland hunting. The act of hunting upland game birds.

vent rib. A rib raised above the barrel by a series of spacers or posts, intended to dissipate barrel heat rapidly.

wad. A physical component of the cartridge that seals and separates the powder from the shot.

wall thickness. The measured thickness of the barrel wall. A minimum thickness is necessary for structural integrity and safety.

whoa. A command used to stop a pointing dog.

wing-tipped. A bird injured in flight but still able to move some distance under its own power.

wingshooting. The shooting of aerialized flying targets or birds.

wrist. The section of the buttstock gripped by the trigger hand.

GLOSSARY 253

Acknowledgments

In essence, this book represents the culmination of twenty years in the uplands. During much of that time, the research was selfishly motivated: many autumn days were spent in the New England woods, just tumbling deeper into this thing that had captured my soul. I suppose I have a whole lot of shooting, a whole lot of missing, and a handful of grouse and woodcock to thank for making me want to decipher the world of upland hunting. I wish, in some ways, that someone else had written this book before me; I could have used it.

I credit Tom Rosenbauer with telling me this book could be written, and that I could write it. I thank Simon Perkins, Steve Hemkens, Dave Perkins, Jordan Smith, Jerry Cacchio, Peggy Long, and Scott McEnaney of The Orvis Company for giving me the opportunity to immerse myself in the world of wingshooting, and to get a backstage pass of sorts, with which guides and dog handlers and shooting instructors and gunsmiths were willing to answer my relentless questions.

Dan Michels, Pat Berry, Thierry Bombeke, Tim and Joanne Linehan, Randy Matis, and Mark Nissen taught me that there will always be more birds than shells, more questions than answers, and when the questions start to get too big, it is best to just go hunting.

Were it not for Ben Holmes, Jim Babb, and Ralph Stuart, I would never have come to consider myself a writer.

Brian Grossenbacher has been a tireless and relentless champion; I've begun to believe that we *all* need one of those, and I couldn't have hoped for a more generous one.

Kim, Willa, and Guppy dealt with me through all of this. Lots of late nights by the woodstove, but I got it done. I am, of course, forever grateful.